GAMERTAG
Stories

First published in 2021

Copyright © Tommy Keough 2021

Tommy Keough asserts the moral right to be identified as the author of this work

ISBN 9798700489829

For George

Lil bits x

Thanks

Mum, Dad, Squish, Big Bro, Big Sis, all my family, Jen, Rich, Bal, Nin, Tommy Hampshire, Michael B, michaelstar* and all my friends who have shown me support over the last years.

This has been interesting journey for me, I would just like to show my appreciation to everyone who has submitted stories and supported this project from the start this is for you.

(Frank Roosen, Frankie, Frankie Roosen)

INTRODUCTION

Gamertags, usernames, online ID, these are some of the words we use for our online gamer profiles. The names we choose to identify our online personas. But why did we decide on the name that defines us online? What made us go "Yeah, that's who I am."

Charging into battle with your squad, or, as a lone warrior, taking that last hairpin corner to win the gold as a professional racing driver. Beating down your opponents to become the ultimate fighting champion. Taking that last hold point and seeing victory scrolling across the screen with your Gamertag illuminated for all to see. The name that will leave a lasting impression on your friends and foes.

So why a book about gamer tags? With the gaming community being bigger, better and stronger than ever before, I feel that now is an ideal time to look at the history behind the Gamertag where did they come from? Why did we pick them? An in-depth look at the gamer tag, which could serve to bring together gamers from all over the world sharing their stories, bringing the incredible gaming community closer together than ever before.

One night while playing Respawn Entertainment's awesome team-based Battle Royale Apex Legends on my PS4 and couldn't help noticing the amount of funny or interesting gamer tags. And it got me thinking How did the individual behind it come up with that name, and has anyone ever done that while playing against me? Seeing my tag and thinking, "Who is this guy? How did he come up with that?" And the conception for Gamertag Stories was born.

Now if you are wondering what my GT is, it's 'Spuff' but more on that later.

Looking at the history of gamer tags you could say the first inception of them was way back in the early days of gaming, in its infancy. The introduction of classic arcade machines such as Space Invaders and Pacman, giving the player the chance to imprint their high score for all to see, by identifying themselves using only three letters. Children of the '80s would pump their loose change into the machine in the hope of getting to change one of the top ten high scores with their initials or if you were like me, trying to write rude words using only three characters. How many of us as kids wished we could make it into the top ten and change the three letters to "POO"? Just me? Whoops, ok, let us move on.

Unfortunately, I was born a little too late to join that initial surge of gaming arcades. With the introduction of home gaming systems from the humble days of Atari in the late 70s and early 80s, the NES in the mid-80s throughout the '90s with the original PlayStation, SNES, Megadrive, N64 as well as many others, Gamertags wouldn't come to fruition. My first use of a Gamertag was in 2000 with a game which would bring online gaming to the forefront of the gaming community and still has a big following over twenty years later: Counter-Strike. Even though there had been many online games before CS 1.6 this was the first one my little fourteen/fifteen-year-old brain had a chance to sink my teeth into and get me completely hooked. I had already been playing games for many years, having a PlayStation, N64 and Gameboy and Game Gear, but none of these let me express my personality for others to see. At that time, I didn't have my PC, but my friends Dave and Rich, brothers who lived two doors down the road did. So many hours of my childhood we would all spend huddled around the warmth of the glowing CRT monitor, shouting, and screaming at the screen trying to get a kill. We would have a fantastic system of one round or one death and then we would rotate and let the next person play. On the off chance it was only two of us playing, sometimes we would let one person use the mouse and control shooting and looking around, while the other would use WASD to move, crouch, jump. At the time, this seemed to work seamlessly. I expect it would not be as easy today.

Counter-Strike 1.6 was originally a MOD for Half-Life, but grew in popularity very quickly, especially considering its time. It was turned into a full game of its own, becoming a powerhouse in the PC gaming community and the basic concept is still going strong today, with CSS (Counter-Strike Source) and CSGO (Counter-Strike Global Offensive). The games are so big that they have been main stayers at Esports competitions for years and show no sign of slowing down.

The late nineties/early two thousands changed forever how gaming was perceived. Before this time gaming was thought of as a pastime that only children and strange middle-aged nerds living in their mother's basement did. It was for nerds and geeks. It wasn't "cool." But with the release of the PS2 in 2000 gaming suddenly became cool, rising to unprecedented levels of popularity.

Even celebrities got on the gaming hype train, fronting adverts, and admitting they were gamers as though previously it had been something to be ashamed of. While in the background people like you and me, had been gaming for years with no shame; it's what we enjoy; it's what brings us together. Being a geek is now incredibly cool and fashionable. Though we did not do it for that: we were gamers through and through.

This increase in popularity gave rise to a lot more people joining the online gaming community, and with the launch of Xbox live in 2002 and PSN in 2006 millions of console gamers now had the chance to express their personalities through choosing a gamer tag, bringing the community closer than ever before. I still remember vividly in late summer 2006 with the PS3 release looming, Sony first announced their full commitment to the online services. having attempted previously with the network adapter available for the PS2 and PS2 Slim. Their new console would come with the network adaptor built-in. Xbox was already ahead of the game at that point, with the release of the Xbox 360 a year earlier. Sony announced that you could register interest in their new online service and choose a username, which would be unique to you. Having gamed predominantly as Spunkmeyer since 2000 on PC when I first started playing CS 1.6 and using the name until I registered for the PSN, I chose the Gamertag 'Spuff' and all this time later it is still the name I use.

With the next generation of consoles and PC gaming being stronger and bigger than ever, the number of gamer tags has reached colossal levels. As of July 2019, there were over 65 million registered tags on Xbox live. From January 2020, over 15 million on Nintendo Switch and Sony have over 103 million active subscribers. Just from console-based gamer tags, that is almost 200 million individuals from all over the world, each with a story to tell. Combine that with the hardcore PC gamers and other platforms, (including mobile, tablet and others) the number of gamers in 2020 in currently... 2.5 BILLION. 2.5 billion gamers across the globe, be it casual gaming or hardcore fans. Gaming is currently the biggest entertainment franchise the world has ever seen. Bigger than movies and music combined and it shows no signs of slowing down. After the disastrous video game crash of 1983, where gaming was incredibly close to dying out, like a phoenix from the ashes it has risen and has become the ultimate entertainment outlet EVER. This means, that over a quarter of the world's population are gamers, with the world's population in 2020 being 8 billion.

A very high majority of those people would have picked a Gamertag at some point, even if they only used it for a short period. So, let's take a look of some of those fascinating stories, and how people came up with the name that defines them online. People from all over the world, who may never meet or have never even spoken to each other in person, can leave a lasting impression with the name they have chosen, I took it upon myself to contact hundreds of gamers to ask them: "What's the story behind your gamer tag?" and here is what a few of them had to say. I'll go first, but before we do that, let's take a look at a list of some of the most popular games which in my opinion may have helped the growth of gamer tags. There are many more examples of fantastic games which helped path the way for Gamertags: this view is purely my own.

(Dualshock 4 + Dreams on PS4)

Space Invaders – 1978 (Arcade Machine)

The game that started it all. The arcade classic that started it all created by Tomohiro Nishikado. Space Invaders was the first arcade machine to utilise the now-famous high score, allowing you to pump in loose change until you could finally achieve arcade legendary status and get your name in the top ten. Shooting the little alien invaders as they get faster and closer to you, trying to wipe them out before the dreaded 'Game Over' screen appears. Having only three characters to choose from, would have made picking the right tag particularly important, so you could gloat to your friends at school and tell them how over the weekend you managed to break into the top 10 and leave your tag for all to see.

PacMan – 1980 (Arcade Machine)

Probably the most famous and recognisable arcade machine video game in history, PacMan took the world by storm in 1980 when it was first released. Developed and released by the video game giant that is Namco in Japan on May 22nd, 1980 and October 1980 in North America. The iconic maze, ghosts and music have made PacMan a household name within the gaming community. Released in arcades two years after Space Invaders and being just as addictive shot PacMan to the top of arcade gaming royalty. Much like Space Invaders, PacMan utilised the three-character method for its top score naming convention.

Quake – 1996 (PC)

In the mid-nineties, attitude was king, and that was no more apparent than in developer id software's mammoth game Quake, released June 22nd, 1996. After the massive success of Doom in 1993, they took it to the next level with fast-paced, multidirectional movement action. I remember going to a friend's house to watch them play (I didn't have a PC at this point.) It was so over the top my eleven-year-old brain fell in love instantly. I feel for many this would have been one of their first introductions to online gaming and what the future holds. With multiple modes available with classics such as team deathmatch and free for all, Quake quickly established itself as a gaming juggernaut, paving the way for the many Quake clones that would follow in the years to come. This is when Gamertags became personal. The ability to write whatever you wanted (within reason) to represent your online persona. The choice was endless, the possibilities seamless. Online gaming was here, and it wasn't going away.

Counter Strike - CS 1.6 - 2000 (PC)

Counter-Strike holds a very special place in my heart to this day, as this was my true introduction into online video games. Originally a Half-Life mod by Minh "Gooseman" Le and Jess Cliffe developed in 1999 Counter-Strike was officially released on November 9th, 2000. Two teams: Counter-terrorist forces VS terrorists. CS was a fantastic showcase for the potential of online multiplayer games. Rescue hostages, defuse the bomb, kill the enemy team, the gameplay was fast, addictive and unpredictable. Many young gamers would have picked their first-ever Gamertag because of this game. A game that is so adored within the gaming community, it has received two remakes over the years in Counter-Strike Source, and Counter-Strike Global Offensive. A massive following, countless mods, Esports, and people still playing the original to this day.

RuneScape – 2001 (PC)

Released on the 4th of January 2001, RuneScape is an MMORPG (massively-multiplayer online role-playing game.) Developed and released by Jagex. Giving the player an entire world to immerse themselves in, with hundreds of quests and NPCs (Non-playable characters) to meet and interact with, Jagex had a giant on their hands. Being a fantasy-based game, this led to a lot more creativity when picking a Gamertag for your chosen character. Rather than the run and gun attitude of many other online games, players felt a lot more invested in their character, levelling up their skills in many different areas, this was an extension of the player themselves, so they would want to choose a Gamertag that could really show their personality... Also, half of 99 is 92.

World of Warcraft -WOW – 2004 (PC)

Another MMORPG that took the world by storm and then some. World of Warcraft was published by Blizzard Entertainment and originally released in North America on November 23rd, 2004 and in Europe on February 11th, 2005. With almost ten million players by 2009 and over one hundred million registered accounts by 2014, WOW is the world's biggest and most popular MMORPG, so much so that the creators of South Park made an episode within the WOW world. This behemoth of a game introduced online gaming to millions, and is solely responsible for millions upon millions of Gamertags... Leeroy Jenkins anyone?

Call of Duty 4 Modern Warfare – 2007 (PS3, Xbox 360, PC)

The first major release to include a whole new era/generation of gamers: the console players. Call of Duty had already been around on PC for a few years and had the previous title Call of Duty 3 appear on the 7th generation of consoles, But Modern Warfare published by Activision and released on November 5th, 2007 changed the face of online gaming forever, bringing with it a tidal wave of new players, all wanting a nice shiny new Gamertag. With console graphics catching up to PC, and fantastic gameplay, this was the moment a lot of people created their Gamertag they still use today.

Fortnite – 2017 (PS4, PS5 Xbox One, Xbox Series X/S, PC, macOS, Nintendo Switch, Mobile)

The Global phenomenon that is Fortnite was released in early access on July 25th, 2017 by Epic Games. Within one year of its release, it had already amassed over 125 million players. Though not the first Battle Royale game, it certainly took its rightful place as king of the BR genre. Being extremely popular with the younger generation of gamers, it spawned millions upon millions of new Gamertags into the world. Still riding high off its incredible success, with new players joining all the time, Fortnite has to be one of, if not the biggest generator of new Gamertags.

Apex Legends – 2019 – (PS4, Xbox One, Nintendo Switch, PC)

Apex Legends, like Counter-Strike, holds a very special place in my heart. Being the game that gave birth to the idea of this very book. Released on the 4th of February 2019 and developed by Respawn Entertainment it was a surprise hit, mainly because there was no prior promotion or knowledge of the game at all. It was announced on the day it was released: within a week the player base was up to ten million (myself included.) and by October 2019 it was up to 70 million players. Much like Fortnite, Apex Legend is a team-based Battle Royal game: you and two friends jump into battle and try to survive 'til the end. This being the time of Battle Royale games, Apex saw a massive increase in popularity, especially as it took its own unique approach, giving each character an interesting backstory as well as their abilities. There is no doubt that Apex Legends help create millions of new and wonderful Gamertags.

Gamertag Stories

(Disclaimer: the rules of the English language don't apply when creating gamer tags, so names may start with a lower case or uppercase, at the user's discretion.)

GAMERTAG BIO

I came up with Spuff in late summer of 2006 and when Sony announced the registration of Gamertags for the upcoming PlayStation network which was to be launched alongside the release of the PS3. Originally, I was called Spunkmeyer for three reasons: one, my love of Spunkmeyer muffins in my early teenage years. Two, as a reference to the character Spunkmeyer in my favourite film Aliens (1986.) and thirdly to entertain my immature childish mentality. After the years passed and the PS3 was due out, I wanted to change my name, but also keep the reference to my old tag as well as my child like outlook on life. I also wanted a short one-syllable word with no numbers or extra characters added in. Something that seems very hard to do now, as most names are taken, and therefore, people have to add in dates or XX ETC. So Spuff was born, short and sweet and a tag I use to this day on PSN. if you are not sure what the meaning is... It's an English slang term for... well, maybe look it up, in fact, probably best you don't...

SPUFF

"Originally, I was called Spunkmeyer for three reasons: One, my love of Spunkmeyer muffins in my early teenage years. Two, as a reference to the character Spunkmeyer in my favourite film Aliens (1986.) And thirdly to entertain my immature childish mentality."

Final Fantasy VII

My all-time favourite game, released by Square in 1997, turned me into a full-fledged gamer. Everything about this game spoke to me, the storyline, characters, the JRPG gameplay, but most of all the music. By far the best soundtrack to any game ever. To this day, I still play it constantly. Be it via PS1, PS3, PS4, PC, PS Vita this will be my number one always.

Metal Gear Solid

Coming out just one year after FF7 this game had me hooked from the moment you press start. Awesome action, amazing stealth sections, and over the top story. For the time on the PS1 it looked fantastic. I saved up my pocket money for ages to buy the special edition with the T-shirt, dog tags, soundtrack and much more. Thirteen-year-old me was a fan, and I still am today.

Uncharted series

If I had to just pick one of the Uncharted games it would probably be 2, or 4, wait... maybe 3? See it's impossible. This is why the entire series makes it into my list. A loveable rouge in the lead, I really wanted to be Nathan Drake. Stunning graphics and some of the best story telling in games ever, make this easy to return to.

Counter-Strike Source

The game that defined me as an online gamer, upon its release back in 2004 bundled with the fantastic Half Life 2. I was blown away by the game. So much so I joined a few clans over the years.

It still holds first place as the most hours spent on a game on Steam.

Resident Evil 3

Keeping it old school, Resident Evil 3 was a fantastic game. Though many prefer Resident Evil 2, which is fantastic, at fourteen I wanted to see as much blood and gore as possible. I still remember waiting outside the shop and asking my dad to go in a buy it, as I wasn't old enough, getting so excited. More zombies, more guns, more explosions. I've replayed this so many times.

Honourable mentions:

Apex Legends, The Last of Us 1/2, Spelunky 1/2, Fallout 3/4/New Vegas, COD: Black Ops 2, Tekken Series, LOTR Battle for Middle Earth, Half Life 2, Skyrim.

Name: Tommy Keough

Instagram: Gamertagstories

YouTube: Spuff Stream

Twitch: Tommysproggler

PSN: Spuff

GAMERTAG BIO

"I probably watched The Fifth Element from slightly too young an age, as I did with most of my favourite films as a small kid; The Lost Boys and Alien along with it. But from the very start, I fell in love with Leeloo's character. She was cute, clumsy and loves food - what was not to like?! Right before I started streaming on Twitch I had been through a very bad patch, I won't go into it, but I felt like I was noticing a lot of very strange signs that I hadn't experienced before, and within a month I had left behind a career and routine that had made me feel like I wasn't me anymore. Painted grey. Zombie mode. I started streaming regularly; Twitch came first and then Instagram happened. I found a place in the gaming community which has been the best thing ever. I've grown as a person, found so many friendships and had a lot of opportunities. Choosing the right name on Twitch felt like a big thing for me. I've looked at so many other streamers for inspiration or to understand how to pick a combination of words that best describes me. I realised that from now on I got to be me. Whom I feel like, who I want to be. Without anyone trying to squash the personality out of me anymore. My real name is Ellie, and with Leeloo being my hero, putting the two together seemed to make sense. I was a bit unsure for a while, but it's stuck and I like it. Sometimes I even get called Leeloo and that's pretty cool too."

Eleeloo

"My real name is Ellie, and with Leeloo being my hero, putting the two together seemed to make sense. I was a bit unsure for a while, but it's stuck and I like it. Sometimes I even get called Leeloo and that's pretty cool too."

The Legend of Zelda: Breath of the Wild

I have never been able to not put down a game like this one. One of my favourite elements in video games is to be able to explore, BOTW gives you that. There is a lot to love about it, it is visually beautiful, and I really love the weapons/ battle system and also collecting ingredients for survival.

Pokemon Soul Silver

My first handheld game was Red, I played Silver, and Soul Silver is just that beautiful remake that I will never tire of and continues to let me re-live the nostalgia and love that I will always have for Pokemon.

Animal Crossing New Horizons

I feel like this game saved 2020 for a lot of people. We were able to socialise, forget out troubles and celebrate annual events at a time where we weren't able to in the real world.

The Witcher 3: Wild Hunt

There are a lot of games that I love in this kind of medieval/ fantasy genre such as the Fable series, Skyrim and Ghost of a Tale; the Witcher ticks all the right boxes for me when it comes to gameplay, mechanics and battle system.

SSX

Aside from handheld gaming, Playstation 2 was the system that started me off becoming a gamer. It was a shared console between my dad, my brother and I, we played through so many great titles. SSX was probably the one that we played the most together.

Instagram: _eleeloo_

Twitch: Eleeloo

Twitter: Eleeloo1

Etsy: Moon Garden Jewellery

a9ce

"I used to trade a lot for gamer tags, on a low level. One day I approached someone who said they knew of someone with a big list of rare gamer tags for sale. I really wanted one, and contacted them, he offered me "G0L" for my Instagram Page. I was really happy and sent the info, expecting him to send me the info for the tag. He took my Instagram and scammed me. I approached the person who told me about him, and he said he was sorry that I was scammed. I asked if he had any tags I could buy or trade for since I got scammed, he felt really bad, but his only tag left was a9ce. And here we are!"

Abstarr21

"My Gamertag is Abstarr21. I chose this because it's basically my real-life nickname but with a spelling variation of Starr instead of Ster."

Ace_of_hearts905/ Gamertown001

"Gamertown001. When I was five my parents bought a Super Nintendo for my brothers, sometimes I played Donkey Kong and Super Mario Bros, then when I was eight, they bought the Xbox original. I played the Prince of Persia trilogy, Fatal Frame 1, 2 and Silent Hill 4. My brother had a PlayStation with Crash Bandicoot and I played this all day in my vacations when I was in the school. In college, I didn't have time to play, but in one class my teacher says "Ok, I need that you do an Instagram profile with your hobbies or whatever you want." The objective was to share your hobbies and see if anyone matched with you. So, I come back to the Videogames. I choose my gamer tag Gamertown001 because my brothers and friends always said to me "ooh she is adorable with her gamertown" and the 001 is because gamertown was already in use. Me and my best friend were coming up with Gamertags to use as our League of Legends account names. We decided to get a deck of cards and use the first card we pick up as our names. He chose the ace of hearts, while I got the queen of hearts. We both added the area code "905" to our name. After he unfortunately passed away from suicide, I took his name "Ace_of_hearts905" and used it for all my consoles to remember him by."

AllieTheGreat08

"My Gamertag is AllieTheGreat08. To be honest, there isn't a big story behind how I chose that. Back in 8th grade, my best friend and I became friends with a small group of guys, and we all hung out constantly. They were huge gamers so all we did was play Xbox together. After months of being "player 2" or just watching them play, we both finally were able to get our own Xbox and we wanted to kind of match our Gamertags. She said, "hey AllieTheGreat08 kind of sounds cool, want to do that?" And I said f**k it and said sure, now I'm AllieTheGreat08. I feel like it's almost like a brand for me now lol. It's my Twitch name, my Facebook page name, it's my name on just about every social media platform and game out there, or AllieTheGr808 if AllieTheGreat08 is too long, or in rare instances, taken."

amk76

"Hi, I'm amk76 because amk - are the first letters of my full name and 76 my favourite number pretty simple."

Amy-Amy-Amyyy

"Hi! My Gamertag is Amy-Amy-Amyyy... but my name is actually Patricia. Nah I'm kidding, it really is Amy. I get so many people asking me what my name is, after seeing my gamer tag, like really. The only reason I chose Amy-Amy-Amyyy is because, when I was setting up my PS3, I had Ruby by Kaiser Chiefs on. I sang along but changing Ruby to Amy instead and it stuck! It's my username for absolutely everything."

AngryPenguin

"My Gamertag is AngryPenguin. It was a name that my boyfriend (now husband) gave to me when we started dating, I've been using it ever since. Penguins are one of my favourite animals, they are cute, and they can be funny/silly much like my personality. Angry came from when I play videogames, I can get heated and catch myself swearing. When I do swear, I guess it's more cute than scary, hence, Angry Penguin."

AtoastedTIGER

"Well, my Gamertag is AtoastedTIGER, I didn't choose it but I do love the Gamertag. I had it since I first started Xbox live back in 2013, if I remember rightly. I wasn't the smartest of kids at the time, so setting an account up I would remember would always end badly because I would forget my details. I had a friend come round and set my account up for me and wrote my details down for my mum to keep hold of; he asked me what Gamertag I wanted, and I said I don't know. This was when he told me he was part of a clan of people who had Atoasted in their name and an animal afterwards. I asked if there are any animals left and he said that one member left the clan and deleted their account. This Gamertag was AtoastedTIGER, this is how I ended up with the name. At first, I thought I'm not going to get any friends with this name. I started off befriending people in the clan who I would play with from time to time and I met some of their friends."

BgameAlot

"Well, that's easy, my name is Brian and I game a lot so... BgameAlot."

GAMERTAG BIO

My name Gamertag -Bigbert0 I have that name because when I was younger, I had an eating problem and for a lack of a better word I got big. Luckily, I didn't get teased much, as I was well-liked by many and usually bullies kept away from me as I fought back. But I've always kept it in my games ever since. I do it to remind myself of how far I've come and what kind of man I've become, how much weight I lost and the determination and physical strength I needed to get there. It's been 20 years having that nickname/Gamertag and it's always the same or a slight variation in all my consoles. Still the same heart, grit and determination but grounded in humbleness.

Big_Bert0z

"I do it to remind myself of how far I've come and what kind of man I've become, how much weight I lost and the determination and physical strength I needed to get there.

The Legend of Zelda: Ocarina of Time

This game blew my mind as a kid, totally infusing everything I loved about gaming, music, immersion, story. It was a revelation when it came out, totally captivated me and sparked my love of gaming and Zelda in particular.

The Legend of Zelda: Breath of the Wild

The only game I played as an adult that made me feel like the kid that played Ocarina of Time. Once again, ahead of its time, amazing gameplay that only Nintendo could provide. It evolved the franchise again in another new unique way.

Metal Gear Solid

The way this story was told, the immersion, gameplay it felt like playing a movie and there was nothing like this at the time. As a teenager this made me look at games as an adult concept if done correctly.

Chrono Trigger

I love RPGs, it's my favourite genre. This game was the beginning of the deep infatuation with RPGs. Story, music and just the grand scale of this game was insane for the SNES.

The Last of Us

The game I show off to non-gamers, of what a game can be. A heart-breaking tale very much pushed the medium forward in storytelling and atmosphere.

They were ahead of the times, they are to this day industry standards and icons in the mediums of video games. Combining music, gameplay, stories, art direction all rolled into some awesome experiences.

Instagram: Pause_gamer

PSN: Big_Bert0z

Cbad21

"Cbad21 - the story behind it is quite simple and unimpressive: I was staying at my cousin's house sometime in the summer holidays during the '00s, as I always did, playing A LOT of Killzone on the PS2. If I remember rightly, you had to each have a profile to be able to play split-screen, so we created them. I still have absolutely no idea how "cbad" was punched in as my profile name that day. Even just a little while after I couldn't remember typing that in, but it stuck, and I still use it to this day! Maybe it's something deep and sentimental about how much fun we used to have hanging out and playing video games when I would go and stay with them. No idea, but that's cbad! Oh, and the 21 is because all the best people are born on the 21st."

Chrononaught

Chrononaught was made when me and my brother got the PS4. My brother and I aren't as close as I wish we were, we fight all the time, have since we were little, even now that I'm nineteen and he is nearly eighteen, we still fight and argue. We were fighting over which Gamertag to choose since our Xbox and PS3 tags were chosen for us, I wanted a unique name, without numbers, at the time my brother wanted one that involved the word fire, and 123 at the end (we were both young when the Ps4 came out) we had never picked a Gamertag before. Finally, my stepdad came into our room and sat with us and simply said "how about Chrononaut" neither of us knew what it meant but agreed in unison that it was an awesome name. Unfortunately, Chrononaut was taken. But we finally managed to take Chrononaught. It felt unique and though it wasn't perfect, it's one of the few things that me and my brother have bonded together over.

Cloudeyboi

"My Gamertag is Cloudeyboi, I picked it when my friend said, "Bruh that clouds is cloudy as fu*k and replied with "Boi, you horny man!"

ClsscNrdyChk

"There isn't much to my Gamertag story, ClsscNrdyChk, I'm nerdy, classic and a chick."

Cole3578

"So, when I was twelve my original Gamertag was crazycoolcole12. I liked it at the time. No judgement! However, my friends would roast me over it. This was the time that all of the big clans took to the scene, Faze, Optix, etc. Me, my brother and two of our friends decided we wanted to start a clan, we decided to go with XxCraZy, I went with XxCraZyReapZz0 Which was the name I stuck with for almost eight years and now, with Clans not necessarily being in the light as much except for FaZe I wanted something more simple, I began playing Pokémon Go and it gave me a randomized name of Cole3578 so, I decided and thought to myself "why not just keep it simple... I landed with Cole3578 and I never looked back really. I still have XxCraZyReapZz0 on my Xbox and my fiancée decided on XxCraZyQueen0 but, my PC tags now stay with Cole3578. It's simple, it's nice and it will do for now!"

(Super Mario Land for Gameboy)

(Predator: Hunting Grounds)

GAMERTAG BIO

I choose this name around 2013-14, there was no deep meaning or even much thought put into it other than I was playing music a lot and considered myself a rocker/metalhead. The confused part was added both because I didn't think myself very smart at the time and my style of gameplay back then would be classed at best "confusing" and unpredictable. After years of playing that's changed somewhat, but even now in games like Among Us, COD Zombies, CIV 5 or any board game, I like to go with the most chaotic options presented rather than sticking to something inherently Good, Bad or Neutral.

Confusedrocker

"The confused part was added both because I didn't think myself very smart at the time and my style of gameplay back then would be classed at best "confusing" and unpredictable.."

Jak 2: Renegade (PS2)

The first game (Jak and Daxter: The Precursor Legacy) was my first PS2 game and was a perfect warm-up to this incredible sequel. It was one of my first open-world third-person shooters and the style of playing fitted me perfectly down to the combat, general style and look and most importantly the story. I can't count how many times I replayed and completed this, the third game Jak 3 was also just as good with even more content, but the story to Jak 2 I loved more.

God of War (PS4)

I never really played the original games on the PS2, but I jumped on this and loved it from start to finish. It was one of the most beautiful games I'd seen, combat was very easy to pick up, the story was amazing and awesome characters with a well-developed fantasy world that made me want to play it again and again.

The Witcher 3: Wild Hunt (PS4)

I played the second Witcher game a little, so I picked this up and struggled to put it down again. The gameplay was difficult at first, but super fun once you got the hang of it, every side or main story quest was interesting, mysterious, and often contained amazing plot twists. The role-playing mechanic where you choose your own story by deciding on different dialogue options was brilliant and added to how customizable your style of gameplay can become. It shouldn't be any surprise that I completed this three times each doing a different character build either going full combat, full magic or full alchemy.

Pokemon Games (Gameboy, DS, 3DS, Switch)

All the Pokemon games in my eyes are fantastic role-playing games. I started with Pokemon yellow and I'm still going strong now with Pokemon Shield. I love the levelling and evolving mechanics, to work hard to make your creatures stronger to the point they become something that looks bigger and more awesome than before. Often the stories aren't hugely impactful or interesting, but I love the basic idea that has been the same since the first few games, which is simply to work to be the best.

Overwatch (PS4)

I've played this the most out of any other online game. I just love how different each playable hero is, pretty much matching any style of combat you prefer. Also, rather than the main matches being just a team deathmatch and concluded by how many kills you got, it's the main principle it's working together to achieve a directive as a team. I also love the mostly upbeat colours of the characters and the surroundings, constantly giving a positive feeling despite the fact you're trying to kill the enemy team.

Name: Billy Poole

Platform: PS4/5 mostly, Nintendo Switch on occasionm also play games on my Mac/PC

Instagram: Confusedrocker

Counterfeitwater

"Counterfeitwater is my most recent username. I got the idea from the YouTuber LazyPurple. One Of his game tags was water 2.0. I thought it was funny, so I put a new twist on it."

cptginge

"The story behind my Gamertag isn't a special one! So cptginge stands for captain ginge. The captain part came from a friend of mine as he also has cpt at the start of his name. So, I needed a name and we were talking, he suggested I start off with cpt too as we are close friends and it's just something we thought was cool. The ginge part came about because of the colour of my hair! So it kind of symbolised me!"

crosshairmedia

"My Gamertag is crosshairmedia, I came up with this name because initially, I was going to make a truther/conspiracy channel on YouTube and expose all the fake news the media pumps out, and how they manipulate us all funded by the powers that be. But I was also into gaming and I love shooters it's what I grew up on like Call of Duty, Battlefield all the old stuff like Black on PS2 and GTA San Andreas so I decided to go with that as my name and that's pretty much it."

DankSpoony

"My name is DankSpoony. Honestly, I was just looking for a

name that's nice to say. A lot of Gamertags are stuff like "XX_ j0sH_Xx" which just sound horrible when you read it in your head. I started looking for soft words and dank is just a clean exhale. The spoon can be dragged on for however long and the Y on the end just came naturally."

Datshitkid/petalsandblood

"I chose petalsandblood for my gaming-page because it kind of combined the two different sides I love, the cute stuff and also the bloody, explicit. I enjoy games like Animal Crossing, where I'm just chilling, watering my plants, go fishing, all that. But I also really enjoy games like The Witcher 3, killing monsters and be a badass. In the past my gamer tag was datshitkid, which I also use for my personal IG and still on PSN (as datsh_tkid), I chose it back then because I am really shi**y at many games, but I still totally enjoy playing them. It's all about the fun for me, not trophies.

GAMERTAG BIO

"Well, my gamer tag is DeadBeatGamer- The reason I picked this is that I knew I was going to create an Instagram account with content, and I knew I'd be streaming eventually which I have recently started. I didn't want a serious gamer tag as I'm quite laid back, I don't take myself too seriously, I love video games but that doesn't mean I'm a pro gamer. So, it popped into my head. I'm a gamer, I'm obsessed with zombie pop culture and I wanted a fun name that could be perceived in many ways so that's what I chose mine."

DeadBeatGamer

"The reason I picked this is that I knew I was going to create an Instagram account with content, and I knew I'd be streaming eventually which I have recently started."

The Last of Us Part II

No idea how I can explain how this is my favourite game of all time and justify it in such a small paragraph so I'll just say this...I can imagine writing a sequel to one of the biggest games of all time must be difficult and terrifying, but Naughty Dog pulled it off tremendously. The graphics are unbelievable, the gameplay was so smooth and so violent but it's the story that gripped me, as it did in the first game. This was the hardest game I've ever had to play as I was uncomfortable, anxious and emotional throughout its entirety. The voice acting in this game is the best I've ever seen. I've never finished a game and sat through the entire credits in tears. The Last of Us Part II is the perfect game for me. It's horrific, it's violent and it's beautiful.

The Last of Us

The Last of Us hit me hard as soon as I took control of the controller. From start to finish, there are so many narrative beats that are perfectly executed with acting from some of the best actors in the industry. There were so many parts of this game that brought tears to my eyes or took my breath away. It's so dark but there is so much beauty in the world of The Last of Us.

Resident Evil 2 Remastered

Resident Evil 2 Remastered ticked every box for me. Remakes are difficult to pull off, especially when they're rebuilt from the ground up, but Capcom did an incredible job here. The graphics, the familiar environments and level design just made the experience so memorable. The original soundtrack option was just the icing on the cake for me too. Incredible!

Silent Hill 2

As a morbid child, I adored all things horror, and the original Silent Hill game was the first horror game I experienced, and I loved it. Silent Hill 2 was everything that the first game was, but better. The atmosphere, the fog, the incredible soundtrack and the general tension in the game is by far the best I've ever experienced. The story was weird and wonderful and even to this day, Silent Hill 2 still holds its own.

Titanfall 2

Titanfall 2 is the best First-Person Shooter that I have ever played. Period. It's almost perfect in every way and gives you the full package. The multiplayer is great and well balanced, and the campaign is the best FPS campaign I've ever experienced! I loved the emotional bond between the Titan BT and Pilot Jack Cooper. Some real Terminator 2 vibes in the story and there are even some Arnold Schwarzenegger Easter eggs in the game!!

Name: Aurie Preece

Platform: PlayStation

Instagram: deadbeatgamer

Twitch: deadbeatgamers

Deku

"Well, my gamer name, as well as my nickname, is Deku, I use NintenDeku because of my passion for Nintendo [fanboy] The name Deku I've had for almost 20 years and I got this nickname from The Legend of Zelda Majora's Mask. When this game came out, a few friends and I would play make-believe using the characters from the game. As much as I like the Goron form of Link, I was always the smallest kid so I was forced to be the Deku form of Link and, as much as I hated it at the time, I was called Deku or Deku Kid from then on."

Dinoaspect7

"My Gamertag is Dinoaspect7 and the reason I gave myself that name is that I was streaming Skyrim one evening with my gang, and I accidentally told them I was a massive fan of dinosaurs. So, they started to create my new Gamertag. A bit lame but I like it."

Dinozloopy_Lou

"Dinozloopy_Lou, because I got called loopy Lou a lot, and I had a clan called Dinoz. Short and Sweet."

DirtyDan9758

My Gamertag is DirtyDan9758, one day, I found a website that I thought was fake and told me I could change my Gamertag for free, what I didn't know was, several months before, Microsoft was offering a free Gamertag change so, I put in DirtyDan as a joke, logged onto my Xbox and, well, it happened.

DoctrUndead

"My Gamertag is DoctrUndead. You see, there is a game that I stream called Dead by Daylight. Anyone who knows me knows that I'm petrified of the doctor. With my love-hate relationship with zombies, I decided to merge the two. DoctrUndead. I've decided to own the two things that scare me the most. I believe this name will stick for the long run. If I were to switch my name to something else, it'd have to do with what I most terrified of...octopus."

(Crash Bandicoot: N Sane Trilogy)

GAMERTAG BIO

The story behind 'DontRachQuit' is pretty simple - my name is Rachel, I love puns, and I have literally zero patience.

I used the tag 'Rachisonfire' for years, which was inspired by one of my favourite bands, Alexisonfire. During the time I was working for UK retail store GAME, I was getting very involved with streaming, both for the store account and my own personal account. As my channel grew and grew, I figured it was time to get out from under the shadow that my name resembled both a popular band and a popular YouTuber's tag (Danisnotonfire) and I tried to think of something new that was both unique and descriptive for my brand.

I've always enjoyed Dark Souls and streaming these games on Twitch has always been a huge part of my content, so I wanted to try and come up with something related to Souls, perseverance, and triumph. When I decided I was happy having my real name involved, and I realised 'Rach' was similarly pronounced to 'rage', the idea hit me like a bolt of Solaire's lightning.

I love that my tag stands for sticking by your goals and continuing to push yourself through a video game until you finally triumph.

It's a shame people often don't instantly understand the meaning of it - I often get called 'Rash' or even 'Rack', and the name doesn't

DontRachQuit

"I love that my tag stands for sticking by your goals and continuing to push yourself through a video game until you finally triumph.

make sense, but it's worth it when people do finally click, as it often makes people smile.

Keep trying, you can do it - Dont Rach Quit!

This is now the tag I use everywhere, for Twitch, YouTube, social media, Nintendo and Xbox. However, I couldn't be bothered switching my PlayStation and Steam usernames over - that stuff takes effort.

My favourite games include, of course, Dark Souls and Bloodborne, The Legend of Zelda series, World of Warcraft, and Pokemon.

Name: Aurie Preece

Platform: PlayStation

Instagram: deadbeatgamer

Twitch: deadbeatgamers

DopeAssDovahkiin

"I mean DopeAssDovahkiin is pretty self-explanatory. I changed my Gamertag, it used to be akaitoxmeiko because I was an anime dweeb who intended to vocalize and that was my ship. Being older and embarrassed and not wanting to lose my stuff to a new profile, I changed it to DopeAssDovahkin because that's what I am. I've loved and played Skyrim since it came out."

DopierShannon

I was about fourteen, so I've had this gamer tag for fourteen years as I'm 28 now. My uncle got an xbox360. Said I could make an account and play when I was over. So I started to make an account, went down stairs to get food and when I came up he had put the name in for me DopierShannon cause he said I was pure dopey, so I couldn't change it then so I had to use it, then as I got other consoles I grew to like the name and have stuck with it ever since a few of my friends in the PS3 days ever put dopier in front of their names.

Drscottmcgluestick

"So, my actual Gamertag is Drscottmcgluestick, This name came about long before the 360 did, which is when I first created it as a Gamertag and used it for gaming ever since. Think it was the early 2000s when I started using the internet, emails etc and the one thing our school drilled into us back in those days was 'never use your real name on the internet'... I'm in Australia btw which is ten years behind the US, and at the time in the state of Western Australia which is ten years behind the rest of the country so had some pretty over-cautious adults around when the internet rolled in. Anyway, so I was sitting at the PC and was asked to enter a name, first was the salutation and I was like well Mr is boring and the next one down was Dr, so I was like sure, why not. I was eating scotch finger biscuits at the time, those awesome ones with the chocolate on the back, so then came to the name Scott. The last name took a while. I was looking around the desk and the first thing that caught my eye was a yellow UHU glue stick, so I was like ok, but the whole thing didn't quite seem right, then my mum had just come home walking from the garage through to the study with McDonald's for dinner... And Dr Scott McGluestick was born. PS yes I was a fat kid growing up."

dumbNunique

Well, my name came up as a joke. I was at dinner with friends. They were making fun of (female) streamers. One came up with "welcome to dumb and unique here is Dominique". I thought it was hilarious, so I went with it and created dumbNunique. Most people react the same way as I intended it, with humour. I usually ignore negative comments since without my channel I wouldn't have met so many amazing people.

Exogeni

"Well at the time I went by Jenni and my favourite videogame was Mass Effect. I'd overheard a random NPC mention Exogeni Corporation and it seemed to fit nicely, like exo-jenni. I started using it as my Gamertag and username for pretty much everything just as a placeholder until I thought of a better name. After a few years it just stuck, now I couldn't even imagine having a different Gamertag. It does vary depending on the platform I'm using but Exogeni is always incorporated".

ExQlusiv-X

"The most recent Gamertag that I've used for years now is ExQlusiv-X, it's my PSN name! I got this name when I first got my PS3 back in the day, and to be fair I'm the worst guy ever in finding a good name. It always used to take me hours to find a good name and if I thought of one it was already in use. The truth about the name is rather funny, about ten years ago there was a certain electronic music style that was big over here in Belgium, called Tekstyle. Many DJs made sets, but never really got anywhere or didn't gain much popularity. I was a fan of this one artist who was good in my opinion. This guy made a set with another DJ called ExQlusiv-X when I was going for a name on the PS3 I was trying everything, and nothing worked. I tried the DJ name, and to my surprise, it worked, and ever since I have used it, it grew on me through the years, and then I started to use it on everything as my username and these days all my gaming friends just know me as ExQlusiv-X. So long story short I just stole it."

Extixe

"Hey, I'm Ryan and my Gamertag was originally Skyl4nder Ry4n, the reason behind it was I loved a game called Skylanders when I was younger. I absolutely adored every second of it, but I've recently changed it, this was because I just didn't play Skylanders anymore and because I was getting bullied for having this gamer tag. That wasn't very pleasant. "Ooh look over there, its Skylander Ryan." I couldn't take it anymore. I recently got a free name change and I changed it to Extixe. I love the name because people keep pronouncing it wrong and it's funny. I also found the name by just typing 5 letters in my keyboard then just editing it a bit."

evilfairie

My Gamertag is evilfairie. I have used it since 2008 when I first got an Xbox 360. My brother from another mother gave it me when he said I had an evil laugh and was short like a fairy. He decided evilfairie would be a good Gamertag. Nine years on I use it for everything including, my PS4 and Xbox One. Now evilfairie is a part of me and I wouldn't change it for the world. I'm a very passionate gamer.

Feistyvixen

"So, my Gamertag is Feistyvixen and my friend suggested it to me. We were just thinking of names, and he came up with that.

A vixen is a female fox, and the feisty part is me apparently! I'm not sure about."

follow8bit

"My gamer tag follow8bit, it comes from where my gaming journey started. Countless hours on the NES playing Mario Brothers or Alex the Kidd on the Master System. Happy times."

Funkertron/ OGfunkertron

my gamer tag is Funkertron. PSN and OGfunkertron on Xbox (Minecraft related.) I chose Funkertron because the name I wanted wasn't available. It was supposed to be funktron, Toe jam and Earls home planet, from the game Toe jam and Tarl. Funkertron was the closest thing and I love transformers anyway So it's a lucky fit. Most people call me funk. Or funkernut or funkertin.

(Nintendo GameBoy)

GAMERTAG BIO

"I started my account recently because I was being accused of being a fake profile on countless occasions... because pretty girls can't/don't know how to game apparently. I wanted to show that not only am I real, but I'm also a big game lover. I play the games and rate them, play with my friends, try new games, I love gaming accessories, superheros, a few anime's and so on. I do all the things most gamers would, I just happen to have a different look compared to most. That ruffles a few feathers with some people, but they get ignored and I try to stay positive. It's crazy and how horrible some people can be because they're sat on a keyboard and not to my face. The first time I played with a group chat, a guy came on and started talking to me saying I was sh*t, we had only just started the game so I'm not sure how he figured that. I took it and took it until halfway through the game I told him he was welcome to leave and he said: "Wow, I didn't know dishwashers could talk". It's crazy the kind of stuff people are comfortable saying just because I'm a female. So in a way, I hope I can make a slight difference in the way girls who game are viewed too."

gamingjoanna

"The first time I played with a group chat, a guy came on and started talking to me saying I was sh*t, we had only just started the game so I'm not sure how he figured that."

Call of Duty - Modern Warfare:

I love FPS games and I've played all of the duty games for a long time!

7 Days to Die:

I love that it's a survival and building game all in one, being able to be creative in the game and try to survive at the same time is so much fun.

Call of Duty - Black Ops 4:

I'm not usually much of a fan of the black ops series but I've enjoyed the recent one with its maps and game modes.

Assassin's Creed Valhalla:

I didn't play any of the AC games until Valhalla came out and my love for Vikings and role-playing games merged into one. Great game!

Borderlands 3:

I enjoy how quirky this game is, it has funny characters with comical phrases, and I love how interestingly different the graphics are.

I play mainly on PC but occasionally on Xbox 1.

Name: Joanna Koetter

Instagram: Joannakoetter

YouTube: JoannaKoetter

Twitch: Joannakoetter

gerezclipz

"I got gerezclipz because people in my area call me Gere and I make gaming clips, so I added them together. Also, I used z because It would make me more unique from other users."

get_switched_on

"My Gamertag is get_switched_on, I came about the name ten years ago. I was going to open up a game shop, but circumstances changed. Eventually, I bought a Switch on day one and quickly decided to go for a complete collection. I started this page sixteen months ago to share my love for all things Nintendo. Seven switch consoles, six hundred plus physical switch games and many more in my retro collection later and here I am."

GhostRiley

"GhostRiley is my Gamertag, I got it as an inspiration from Ghost, one of the Call of Duty characters."

Goemonster

"My Gamertag is Goemonster. The name came from a cool Japanese live-action movie called "Goemon". The story is a bit similar to the tale of Robin Hood. Goemon itself is quite popular among Gamertags, so I thought it would be fun to make a play on words to make it something like "Goemon-ster". Although the pronunciation is often confused and mispronounced, it is fun to hear everyone say it differently."

gsxaaron

"I have a GSX-R motorbike and I'm called Aaron, nice and easy, gsxaaron."

hades2585

My Gamertag is hades2585. How I got my Gamertag is through one of the worst days of my life, so I've been epileptic from the age of eight, I'm now thirty-four and always had a hard time with it. When I was in my twenties' I had a really hard time to the point where my local hospital put me into an induced coma, which I was in for two weeks but in that time I had died four times, the longest I was dead for was three mins and twenty-one second they brought back to life, the doctors that were looking after me was a big gamer and was talking about games. He really helped me as I was in a really bad place, and he said if I get better and stop having epileptic seizures, he would buy me a console. I didn't believe him just thought it was to give me something to focus on. I got better and on the last day of me being in hospital the doctor came in with a brand new PS3 and a handful of games, I couldn't believe it. He said to me that I was really lucky and he couldn't believe how many time I had escaped hades clutch, unless you are hades, then told me to enjoy it and we have been good friends ever since.

GAMERTAG BIO

"Well, the reason I chose this tag was because I was writing a book about me and my father when I was a child. He passed away when I was nine in '92 so the book covers the original 35 games I still have of his. Whether good or bad I reviewed those games, but also the story behind. I then decided to create an IG to kind of get the word out. Every game I review has a little back story about me, or friends and family. So, The_Chronicles_of_a_Gamer was born, chronicling all the games I've ever played in alphabetical order. My actual gamer tag is on PSN its Handsome_Rob_7 because I'm handsome, my name is Rob, and my favourite number is seven."

My PlayStation tag, I choose this because when I hit my sophomore year in high school, I had severe acne and all girls started to make fun of me. Once I hit my senior year the acne went away and now all the girls started to call me Handsome Rob which I found funny because everyone called me Bobby. Unfortunately, Handsome Rob was already taken so I added underscores and my favourite number 7 at the end, and so Handsome_Rob_7 was created.

THE_CHRONICLES_OF_A_GAMER

Handsome Rob 7

"My PlayStation tag, I choose this because when I hit my sophomore year in high school, I had severe acne and all girls started to make fun of me."

Contra

I picked this game because it was the first game I beat with my dad and it definitely had sentimental value and I play it every year. Believe it or not, I can beat it without the Konami code, without dying and under 15 minutes.

NHL '94 (Sega Genesis)

I picked this because I loved this game growing up and it was the same year that Mark Messier delivered the Stanley Cup to my city of NYC for the New York Rangers. I played this for years on end and even played it at my high school and beat everyone who challenged me throughout the day. It was an amazing day and an awesome memory.

Resident Evil

I picked this because I was absolutely in awe during that opening scene and seeing that first zombie turn its head was pure terror. The polygon graphics, narrow and tight camera angles with a phenomenal soundtrack made this game special. I love horror and this game had everything! Blood, gore and zombies. The mansion and all the secrets in it will never be forgotten.

Skyrim

I picked this because this was all I played until that shiny platinum popped. I lived and breathed this game for months putting in about 315 hours. I was so into this game that when I was ducking and being sneaky I physically ducked too, that's how insanely into this game I was. It was an epic adventure that holds an epic experience.

God of War (PS4)

I picked this game because I was in love with the franchise for all eight games since it was released on the PlayStation 2. I was in a bit of shock and thought that they are beating a dead horse when I heard yet another game was being released. However, all that quickly changed when I learned he was leaving the Greek

Parthenon and moving on to the Norse Parthenon. The old lore mixed with the new lore and vastly different gameplay was the freshness it needed. It was a great story that made me shed a tear (or two) when it was over.

Name: Rob

Instagram: the_chronicles_of_a_gamer

PSN: Handsome_Rob_7

homeless_pigs

"My Gamertag on most things is homeless_pigs and it's because back on Xbox 360 I found a friend on Minecraft (this was the first time we ever talked back in 2013) And we were making a theme park. I decided to make a game where you had to race up ladders inside of a pig and I gave it a little hat. I wanted to change my Gamertag because before it was "IlovedanTDM." I know, I know, I was 8, so I settled on homeless_pigs and have never gone off of it. Me and my friend still talk to this day."

(Super Mario Land for Gameboy)

(PS Vita playing Final Fantasy 7)

GAMERTAG BIO

"Okay, so now I have a minute I can tell you the rather silly story of my Gamertag... So, early in high school, we had a substitute teacher, and the poor guy was obviously new to the job and incredibly nervous. For some reason instead of starting to call the register alphabetically, he jumped into the middle to my name, Parry. Halfway through saying it he realised his mistake and swapped to the start and ended up saying "Pazreen" the other kid's name was Azreen. So as a result, I ended up being called Pazreen for a while, which eventually got shortened to just Paz. Fast forward to when I got a console that you needed an online tag for and it seemed natural to just go with HUWPAZ, and that's been my Gamertag for years and years now!"

HUWPAZ

"So, early in high school, we had a substitute teacher, and the poor guy was obviously new to the job and incredibly nervous. For some reason instead of starting to call the register alphabetically, he jumped into the middle to my name, Parry. "

The Last of Us:

Naughty Dog were a company pushing the boundaries of video game story telling for a while before this game hit and then they blew the doors off with this game.

There's barely a wasted moment, everything has a reason for being and even the briefest appearances for characters give you a taste for who they are and that's down to people excelling at their craft. Oh, and also, THE GIRAFFES!

Portal 2:

This game is a masterwork of clever design and extremely simple ideas executed perfectly. Incredibly challenging, super rewarding and often hilarious, this game is a joy. That song at the end, Still Alive, will always stick in my mind!

Overwatch:

I am a HUGE Overwatch nerd. I'm a big fan of shooters and throw in some superb objective based modes and an incredibly broad range of characters with awesome abilities and you're likely to have a game I'll love.

I've experienced some of my favourite moments in gaming thanks to Overwatch, it's got a special place in my heart.

Diablo III:

Who doesn't love a good bit of dungeon crawling?!

Diablo III, whilst lacking the serious depth of its predecessors, was a game that clicked with me instantly. Some seriously cool character classes, fun stat min/maxing and HUGE boards of enemies to slay meant this is a game I still go back to.

The Legend of Zelda: Breath of the Wild:

What an utterly jaw dropping achievement in game design and an amazing experience as a gamer BOTW was. So much deeper than it looks at face value with scope for some serious inventive moments as a player (I think even more than Nintendo intended!) and a world teeming with life. If there's ever a game that launches with a console that betters this, I'll be amazed!

Instagram: deadbeatgamer_huw

Twitter: h_paz

Twitch: deadbeatgamers

itsLovec

This all started around 2011 when I got my first Xbox. I picked a generated name and it gave me TackledShoe797. I was young around the time and I was always watching YouTube and wanting to become a YouTuber one day. I then got a Roblox account around August of 2011 under the name Babbaganeuw I stuck with those two names for a little until I decided to change it to MadWolfGamer797 that was around 2014. I eventually got an Xbox one around 2015 and kept the name. But then I found a game called Geometry Dash on my phone. I was glued to it 24/7 and eventually gave up playing on the Xbox as well as on Roblox, I grew out of that around the beginning of the year. I decided to make my name AmazingDemon. I made it this because some of the hardest levels in the game had a difficulty of "Demon" and I beat a good number of them and soon that's where I sat for half a year. Around late 2014 I changed it to Xkham, and that found a good spot until I forgot my password for Geometry dash and changed it to Xkhaum. In 2016 I got my first PC that I still use daily! My name Xkhaum was everywhere! Discord, Steam, Geometry dash and even YouTube. I started to play a game called Rocket League and joined a friends team called T1 Tactical 1mpact. It was a joke team so I had T1 in front of my name. I was in a buddy's stream one day and he called me Tixkhaum because I had the T1 and he thought it was an I. I liked it then changed everything to that. Then I started to get into content creation with the name in August of 2018. I loved the name, the vibe of my content it was all going well until early 2019. I was in a huge phase of doubt and decided to rebrand. I wanted a name that suited my actual name and what I wanted my content to feel like. I wanted to spread love to all who I met during this adventure, I wanted to entertain those of all ages and even motivate and help those no matter the cause. I went into google translate and put my name into the English part and started searching. I was searching for only 5 minutes to stumble on a Slovak word called "Lovec" That was it I thought to myself. At the time websites were not being nice and would not allow me to be named Lovec even though there were no accounts called Lovec. So I did what I thought was smart and put an "its" behind it. It sounded better than before. And eventually, when I am recording content like I always wanted to do since I was young back in 2011, I can be like "Hey guys! itsLovec here...

Jeannray

"So my gamer tag is Jeannray, it's a play of my name, Jeanneret pronounced john-ray"

GAMERTAG BIO

"Well, I wanted my name to be included. And I love old school and new games. And back in the day, 'arcade' was a place you could go to enjoy gaming. So Jessicas_arcade contains all the games that I enjoy playing. Old and new. I hope to stream soon as well, for then people can virtually hang out with me in my arcade."

There are quite a few games that shaped my love for gaming growing up, they may not be my top favourites, but I think it's important to list them.

NES was the console I grew up with, my dad bought it for himself, and once I was finally old enough, I gave it a go, I wasn't always very patient with it, but I loved it nonetheless.

Super Mario Bros. with Duck Hunt was the first game I ever saw and experienced, it has the most nostalgia for me. The Legend of Zelda. I mostly watched my dad play. Zelda was one of the NES games that had a secret way of saving your progress. He had almost completed it when my friend and I decided to play it, and well, we didn't save it correctly. Let's just say my dad never completed it. I felt so bad I made him a tiny Link figure from clay. That soundtrack is one that will always fill my heart with memories. We didn't own Tetris, but we owned Tetris 2, that was one of the games I was able to master at a young age. Like I mentioned before, we only had an NES system,

Jessicas_arcade

"There are quite a few games that shaped my love for gaming growing up, they may not be my top favourites, but I think it's important to list them. "

but my best friends brother had a Super Nintendo, and it drove her crazy when I always wanted to play Street Fighter 2. Her brother hated it even more when I would beat him, 'cus we both knew that I didn't know what I was doing. In my teens, my dad bought some games for our computer that we would play together. Myst was a favourite, I loved taking notes that I found throughout the game in order to solve all of the complicated puzzles. And old school Tomb Raider with the boxy triangular Lara started my love for Tomb Raider. Lara Croft will always be one of my most loved game characters.

Mass Effect trilogy (PC)

These games completely brought back my passion for gaming in a way I could have never imagined. I was blown away by the character customization, the story and my ability to make choices, and how my choices strongly influence my character and gameplay. I had never experienced such an immersive gameplay experience before. The replayability is insane, I always have an ME game going!

Fallout (PC) (3, New Vegas, and 4)

As a sucker for character customization, I, of course, loved that in these games as well, but the whole retro and atomic bomb storyline is so creative, it gives an amazing setting for these games. I love the expansive open world and creative NPC's I come across. These games are just a blast, and I easily spend hours and hours on end playing them. I never get tired of replaying Fallout.

The Longest Journey Series (PC)

I love the story, characters, and world that this game takes place in. The original game is quite outdated, but I still love it and wish they would remaster it. This was the first game where when I was playing, it went back and forth between playing as different characters, being able to see the story from different sides. This series is extremely underrated and doesn't get the love it deserves. A mix of modern, dream and fantasy worlds. I hope more people discover it.

The Last of Us Series (PS4)

I played both games for the first time in 2020 during the quarantine. I bought my first PlayStation specifically to play these games. I hadn't read much about the games, but I knew the original had gotten extremely high reviews (and of course the second one had not been released yet). The opening news announcement in the game where it's talking about a virus outbreak was so eerie since we were currently being locked down from an unknown virus ourselves. I did not know this game was about a zombie virus, so the timing of playing this game was insane and comically perfect. It sucked me in right away and I hardly left my couch. The graphics, story and gameplay where amazing. I didn't expect to fall in love with the characters so much. And let's just say, the second game had my emotions reeling in a way that a game has never made me feel before. Masterfully done in my opinion.

Tomb Raider

I have to choose Tomb Raider! I have not played all of them, but I did play a handful of the originals and most of them after 2007. I love Lara as a character, and it never gets boring swinging from cliffs and raiding tombs! And although Lara's background story never changes, they always somehow figure out how to make each new game follow a fun adventure and intriguing storyline.

Other honourable mentions: Skyrim, Bioshock, Half-Life, Uncharted, Broken Age.

Name: Jessica

Instagram: Jessicas_arcade

JimmylCarr

"Well, my Gamertag is JimmylCarr. The reason behind it is because Jimmy Carr is my favourite comedian."

joshibear

"So, my ex actually came up with my name but I like it that much I just haven't changed it. Now it's my name on everything, it's meant to be pronounced "joshibear" but because we used to say it weirdly (because why not) it's now joshibyar."

Joshny

"So, the story behind it is quite simple. Since my name is Joshua, my nickname is Joshny. I wanted to have a more exciting name, but I thought it would be perfect, as most of me call it that."

Kadust

"My name comes from a made-up word by a kid in kindergarten from when I was three. This strange kid I was friends with made-up this random sound/word Kadust and started calling me that. She called me that for a few years and I've just used it online as it has always been free seeing as it has no meaning or background. Kadust.Universe just came in because on this Instagram I am sharing my Universe, but my Gamertag everywhere is Kadust where it was not taken."

katikaiei

"My username is basically my nickname I had it since I was thirteen years old, it will sound silly but if you say candy in Greek "katikaiei"(I'm originally from Greece) it sounds like you are saying something is on fire! In English is just plain candy + k, the K is my initial."

Kayip_c_gaming

"Well, my name is my name, Kayip is my first name and c is from my last name. My name means family profession and my dad used to have a restaurant where I worked two-thirds of my life in it, so you can kinda say I did the family profession."

Kennyswar

My gamer tag is Kennyswar, Kenny was my nickname growing up amongst friends, but the war part is derived from a band name idea I had. When I was eighteen/nineteen I was jamming with a few friends as a vocalist and we were going to name the band "FaithsWar", hence Kennyswar. The FaithsWar name came from the ideology of faiths that leads to constant wars throughout history.

KINGBLACKDRA

It's pretty simple how I got my username, when I was young, I loved playing RuneScape, I was so addicted to the game but then I found a first-person shooter called Combat Arms and

I needed a username for it. I had a couple of accounts on there and I realised I needed a username for a main account so I was sitting with a friend and just brainstormed for some names, I came up with Fireking, dragonking and a few others which I can't remember, but they were all used in the game, but one of them was Kingblackdragon the problem was that you could only fit in 12 characters in your name so my name became KINGBLACKDRA and I stuck with the name until. I got the Gamertag around 2012 and I'm really happy with the name because I don't have any special characters in it, like a 4 instead of an A.

Kinglizzard/ King_lizzard

"My Gamertag is Kinglizzard on Xbox King_lizzard on PS4. In my younger years I was very sporty, at one point I was road racing, mountain biking, and playing tennis. A few of the people I rode with and played tennis with noticed that when the going got tough my tongue would hang out my mouth. After a short while, they started calling me Lizard making jokes that I was trying to catch flies. Later on, someone added the "king" and that's what friends called me for a while. I always joke it was because I was cool, but that's the real story. Anyway, when I brought my Xbox360 I just added the extra "z" to my Gamertag to be different. As it happens now, I suffer from a lot of health issues and this Gamertag just reminds me of better times when I was ultra-fit and carefree".

kingmuadzam

"I got this name back in 2015 when I was playing Clash of Clans Clash of Clan or COC for short, uses a king system so I thought why not name myself as king and muadzam is currently a city I live right now so I combine it and BOOM "kingmuadzam" Everybody calls me muadz or king since then."

Kirbydance

When creating my Steam account, I felt that my previous Gamertag was more of something for me and my sibling, my computer was for me and me alone. I wanted it to reflect me. My friends who had been playing PC for years had cool names with cool stories. They played League of Legends a lot, and I needed a name that I'd be happy with and never wanna change. For my profile picture on discord, I had a meme involving the lovable Nintendo character Kirby. I thought it was funny and Kirby was one of the few games I played when I was young on the DS. Whenever awkward situations would occur in my little group of friends, I'd always put in chat the Kirby dance emoticons...

<(°.°<) (^°.°^) (>°.°)>

...To break the tension.

And so, my friend suggested Kirbydance be my Gamertag for Steam and League. Though I don't play PC games as much as I used to due to work and college, I'm always proud of my Gamertag in the few PC moments I do get.

KJoCon

"My Gamertag is KJoCon My platform is Xbox. My Gamertag is my full name, just shortened: Kieran James O'Connor = KJoCon but it's not the name I was born with My name was Kieran Scragg. My therapist at the time thought it might help me bury the childhood trauma that is in my past. Plus, Scragg is a damn awful name aha."

KryptoKnight

"My Gamertag is KryptoKnight and it came about from a few different influences. I've played guitar since I was twelve and Kryptonite by 3 Doors Down was the very first song I learned completely and is still a favourite. I'm also a big DC fan, especially Batman, and loved the iterations where he takes on Superman with Kryptonite weapons and armour which is where I got the Knight idea along with the fact that as a gamer I prefer to play as the good guy."

Ladonnarossa

"My Gamertag is Ladonnarossa. in English it is "the red woman" I picked it because many of my friends call me this, it is a kind of nickname. The fact that I have red hair and I always wear red, quite intuitive, nothing special but I love it, "ladonnarossa" has become my geek alter ego."

LadyMobesh

"My Gamertag is LadyMobesh It is my magic given name. Mobesh is my granted magic name given and Lady denotes me as a high priestess. My family come from an ancient line of what Is known as druids. I am both Celtic and Nordic, with Asian. Therefore, Lady Mobesh Laithis is my complete title as a druid for my cultures. I use my magic name because it is a token of good luck and good fortune."

lecrii

"I came up with the username lecrii because I used to use discord a lot and there is a saying which means I'm sad or that made me sad which is le cri. I thought of that and put them together which made lecri and I wanted something more because. It looked quite short so as all gamers do. I put an I on the end."

Legroomgaming

I did have to "realign" them across PSN and XBL a while ago. I was initially 'Legroomgaming' on PSN but 'Groomgaming' on XBL as it wouldn't let me have Legroomgaming despite it being free. I had to wait from Day 1 of owning my PS3 (Easter 2008) until Sony brought in the PSN ID change feature in 2018 to get one Identity across both.

LienSue

"My Gamertag is LienSue and I chose it first in an online MMORPG (GW2). "Lien" is the name of a white dragon from one of my favourite books back in my childhood. And Sue is my general nickname, so, this one was a logical take."

LiiDOW

"My Gamertag on pretty much everything is LiiDOW. LiiD was created by taking the first letter of a song from the anime Initial D that I liked, "Love is in Danger." The OW came from the main game I play, Overwatch. combine the two, and you have my Gamertag."

lilkong1992

"My surname is Monk, my Gamertag is lilkong1992, because King Kong is huge, I'm a 6ft man, tiny compared to King Kong. so lil kong and 1992 was the year I was born so lilkong1992."

Liquid chalk

"Not sure if my Gamertag story is that interesting. Liquid chalk came about when I made my second PSN account. I looked for inspiration around me and saw a liquid chalk pen and BAM. Stuck with it, I've thought about changing it but it's pretty unique, so now it's me. I am chalk, liquid chalk."

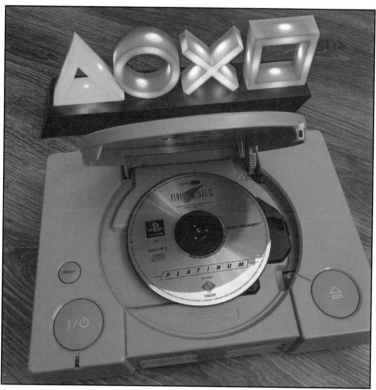

(Original PlayStation)

GAMERTAG BIO

"I don't have a special story about how my Gamertag came about. I've been gaming online starting with COD MW2 from the age of ten. I can't remember the Gamertag I had but I had it for a long time until a few years back. Then I changed it to Lucky_Tobi99. Most people think my name is Tobi but it's my last name and 99 is the year I was born. The funny thing is with Lucky is that I just thought it sounds fairly good with Tobi."

My name is Naomi Tobi, I love so many games that it was pretty hard to choose my top 5. What I quickly realized is that all my top 5 games are PlayStation Exclusives:

- The last of us (both part 1 and 2)
- Horizon Zero dawn
- God of war
- Days Gone
- Spider-Man

Name: Naomi

Instagram: lucky_tobi99

Lucky_Tobi99

"I've been gaming online starting with COD MW2 from the age of ten. I can't remember the Gamertag I had but I had it for a long time until a few years back."

MACCAgames

"Mine is simple... my middle name is Maccarini... and I love games, so MACCAgames."

Makama

"Hey! Mine's Makama, pronounced "Mah-Kah-Mah" and it came about from my baby cousin who couldn't pronounce my real name. So, he called me Makama one day, and it just stuck with most of the family since then."

MarkAndExecute

"My gamer tag is MarkAndExecute on Xbox. I'm a big Splinter Cell fan and the name is derived from a gameplay mechanic that was introduced in SC: Conviction. When I saw the demo, I was blown away by how cool and badass it looked so I decided to adopt the name."

Mastertimos

"Here's my story: The year was 2001. I was twenty and I had just finished serving my two years in the army and I was a college Freshman. Those two years pulled me away from gaming which was mostly in the form of PC gaming. Then, my older brother goes and buys this gaming console called "Xbox". I had no idea what that was about, but he did invite me over to his place to check it out. He bought a bundle with two games included... Ninja Gaiden and Hitman. We ended up playing for hours and hours on that day and I was blown away! For the next few months, I'd finish up my college classes and would go straight to his place, even when he wasn't at home! He knew how crazy I was about video games and even gave me his spare key. As a young man, getting ready to enter society as an independent man, I wanted to have an Xbox of my own. I got myself a part-time job alongside my studies, and a few months later I went to get my very own Xbox console. I bought a bundle together with a little racing game.... ...called Project Gotham Racing. But as I was browsing the game shelf, I noticed a funny looking game with a guy in a suit and mask called "Halo: Combat Evolved". Though hesitant at first, I thought it wouldn't be a bad idea to grab an extra game. Who knew that little game would define the gamer I am today? The Master Chief was my new hero! He was the coolest guy I had seen in a video game and that's coming after having played Ninja Gaiden with the mighty Ryu Hayabusa being the main character! Halo 2 followed three years later and I just couldn't get enough of the Master Chief kicking alien butt! And one year later, the Xbox 360 is released! And along with it, an online service called Xbox live that required a subscription and a Gamertag! It literally took me just a split second to decide that the online world of Xbox would know me as Mastertimos! Fifteen whole years have passed from that day and I still have and use the same Gamertag! Never crossed my mind to change it or to start a new account, even once! Even when I got hacked in 2011, I patiently waited for Microsoft to retrieve my account and return it to me.

MissHorror13

"My Gamertag is MissHorror13, I've been using it since the PS3 got released back in 2006/07. I was in my early teens and OBSESSED with all things horror. Movies, games, I even had a Nightmare on Elm Street playing cards when I was eleven. I loved the creativity that came with all the "bad guy" characters. (Freddy was always my fav.) I was one of those weird kids who never had a childhood fear, so I could always appreciate a really good horror movie or horror game and not be scared to watch or play it. Halloween was also always my favourite time of year. My mom would make these dummies out of my dad's old work clothes, stuff them with newspaper, put a scary mask & some fake blood on them and as a toddler, I would sit on their laps and call them my "friends." I have just always loved the blood and guts movies & games and thought the gamer tag suited perfectly. 13 is my also favourite number so I added it on the end to make it perfect!"

MituDjakarian

"So my 'Gamertag' is "Mitu Djakarian" or "mdjakarian". Anyway, the 'Mitu' part is because when I was a kid, I used to say "I love you!" to my parents every night before going to sleep and my mom would reply "Me too!". I always liked the sound of it so one day I was going to create an account on a website and needed a nickname, so I thought 'Mitu'(me too) would be a nice idea (in Portuguese, my native language, 'mitu' would read as 'me too' in English). The website had a forum so I met other people and they would call me Mitu and the name stuck with me. Then, when I was a teenager, I was obsessed with System of a Down. I read everything I could find about them and since they are Armenian, I read about the country as well — their culture, their history, etc. I also tried to learn a bit about their language, and I learned that Armenian family names always end in -ian or -yan, which means "son of". Since my family name in Portuguese literally means "rabbit", I thought it would be cool to try to translate it. So, I found a website that said that rabbit was something like 'djakar' or 'chagar' so I then added the -ian and got the Djakarian. I started using both the names together and that's how Mitu Djakarian came to be. It's my internet name to this day, sometimes shortened to 'mdjakarian'."

Monumenty

"Monumenty came from a little amalgamation of a name "Monument Cola" which I was inspired to make from a PewDiePie video back when I was 12 years old. He said that his username came from the things he loved, so did the same — I combined Monument Valley and Coca Cola into one — Monument Cola — but that's normally too long, so I shortened it to Monumenty."

MrPoshShark

"Good day dear readers I am MrPoshShark and the story of my Gamertag is a tale of bitter irony which I sincerely hope will provide a small giggle. Many a year ago I had a simple

GT (surname and numbers, woe is me) one day I decided to change, but what to pick? Well one of my favourite idioms was how my real name was common as muck, so I figured "Posh" was a suitably ironic start, but this was merely the first of a multi-layered masterstroke of irony. You may be surprised to find out that I am mortally afraid of open water. If I ever saw anything in a body of water, I would rather learn how to fly rather than stay in the water, so I figured shark. I found out shortly after settling on the MrPoshshark mantle that I suffer from a rather rare (and a total pain in the arse) allergy known as Aquagenic urticaria... simpler known as a dermal allergy to WATER."

MRTheChez

"MRTheChez. Honestly, I wanted a Gamertag that said, hey that is me, Chesney. I did not want any numbers, just a short Gamertag. I bought my ps3 back in 2011, setting up the console successfully, but then it asked me to set up a Gamertag, I sat there on my couch for five hours straight and I couldn't come up with anything. Suddenly it just popped into my head, MRTheChez (a.k.a Trophyhunter) and ever since then it became my gaming identity, I still love it."

Ms_Beeka

"My name is Rebecca and Gamertag is Ms_Beeka. I've been gaming since I was young. I had never played online until around 2015 on my PS3. I am terrible at thinking of unique names. A common nickname of mine is Becca. Eventually, one of my siblings started calling me Beeka or Rebeeka. I added "Ms" in my Gamertag as well. Thus Ms_Beeka was born!! In 2018, I moved onto the PlayStation 4 and stuck with the same Gamertag. And now, my Gamertag is also my YouTube Channel's name."

Muffinboy

"I love muffins, and anything sweet and once when I was really small maybe three or four, I took a few muffins from a store without telling the owner. They laughed so hard they called me the muffin boy and that's been my nickname ever since. So it's not only become like a gamer tag but my real nickname with loved ones as well."

GAMERTAG BIO

I've always been an avid gamer, right back from when I was around eight or nine, playing on friends' Commodore 64's and BBC Micros! We were never allowed computer games as a child, so that's where I got my fix. My first PC was in 1995, and I played Laser Squad, Eye of the Beholder, and the seminal Tie Fighter. I was already a huge Star Wars fan, so this was right up my street! Such an awesome game, flying around and destroying rebel scum! Still one of my all-time favourite games. Fast forward a few years, I started playing online games, so I needed a tag. I took my inspiration from my favourite Star Wars character, Boba Fett. On his left pauldron, he has a small skull symbol of some fantastical beast. That beast is a Mythosaur, and so I adopted this as my online moniker! I've used it ever since (with the exception of when I played Day of Defeat in a clan, where my name was Major Dope!).

Mythosaur

"I took my inspiration from my favourite Star Wars character, Boba Fett. On his left pauldron, he has a small skull symbol of some fantastical beast. That beast is a Mythosaur, and so I adopted this as my online moniker!"

Tie Fighter, Total War series, Xcom (original and the new versions,) Baldurs Gate, FF7, Destruction Derby 2, GTA, Shinobi 3, Goldeneye, Tenchu Stealth Assassin, Alien Breed (original) and so many more!

Can't explain why I love these and so many more games, they just hook me. I think it's all about escapism, losing myself in another word, or another experience that I could never do in real life.

Name: Duncan

Instagram: dunkish79

Napalmsatan

"Napalmsatan, I was the girl who grew up with big brothers only, and all my best friends as a teenager were heavy metal listening b**tards! I chose Napalmsatan because it reminded me of a Municipal Waste gig back in 2009 I'd never been so happy in my life. Screaming my lungs out trying to repeat their lyrics."

NastyKelly

"My Gamertag NastyKelly is inspired by my boyfriend's Gamertag NastyScorp and when we play together, I'm happy to show we're a gamer couple, and the nasty part came out an old gamer clan he was in."

Nebb

"My Gamertag is Nebb, it started with me wanting a space-related Esports name, so it started as Nova, I didn't like this very much, since a lot of people had it, already so I switched to Nebula. I got a creator code with this but it was too long of a Gamertag so I changed my Fortnite creator code to Nebb, and so my name has stuck ever since, even my friends started calling me it."

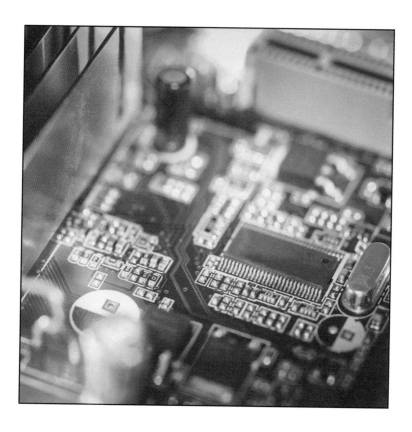

GAMERTAG BIO

"Neko_Wildfire: My gamer tag came from when I was starting a new Skyrim save and I was thinking of a name for my Khajiit. I'd thought about a lot of names cat-related, searched the internet then I came across the word 'Neko', which is Japanese for cat. I thought it was a wicked and unique word, so I called my Khajiit Neko! When I started gaming with people on Twitch, Instagram and Twitter, I didn't have a gaming name, so it started with my Khajiit and love for Skyrim! I also love cats and all animals. I have a crazy cat myself (Lulu) and everybody loves to see her on social media and streams! I'm a very independent and free-spirited person, some say wild with a bit of attitude... So, I added wildfire to the end and BAM! That's how I became Neko Wildfire!"

- The Elder Scrolls V: Skyrim

- Stardew Valley

- The Witcher 3: Wild Hunt

- Call of Duty Warzone

Neko_Wildfire

"When I started gaming with people on Twitch, Instagram and Twitter, I didn't have a gaming name, so it started with my Khajiit and love for Skyrim!"

Skyrim

Every time I start a new playthrough, it's as exciting as when I started the first one 8 years ago!

Skyrim is the perfect escape from reality for me and I've spent hundreds of hours getting lost in the land of Skyrim, hunting dragons and their souls, new quests and loot.

It's such a vast land with so many options to play the stories how you want them to and at your own pace, it's always been my number one game. Plus, you can play as a badass Khajiit. What's not to love?!

Name: Lauren

Instagram: Neko_Wildfire

Twitter: Neko_Wildfire

Twitch: Neko Wildfire

Nenet

"My Gamertag is Nenet and my name is Nerea. I changed the letters Nere-nene, then added one more letter, Nenet. I like Animal Crossing."

NeonSw1ft

"My friend who is in love with Fortnite made a clan called Neon and I was invited to be the Co-host, and that was the reason for NeonSw1ft."

NintendoSwitch86

"NintendoSwitch86. I picked the name because I'm a huge Nintendo fan and I have been since the NES days, I currently own about 300 Switch games, both standards and collectors' editions. Contrary to what most people believe, the "86" part of the name is not my birth year. I picked 86, because it rhymes, but also as a tribute. On September 27th, 1986, my favourite bass player died. Cliff Burton, who played bass on Metallica's first three albums. I'm a bass player myself, and also a recording industry major. I was in a band for nine years called Skullkin. Since then, I needed a creative outlet, Instagram and gaming has provided that for me with NintendoSwitch86."

NoScoobyD0nt

"My gamer tag is NoScoobyD0nt The story behind it isn't that amazing but my brother always controlled all the consoles, so when I finally got my own Xbox I was pretty stumped. At the time I was just getting into cosplay and dressed up as Velma quite frequently and I offhandedly said Scooby-Doo. My brother said it was lame and told me it should be Scooby don't. I loved it so much that I used it for my Gamertag."

OhGoodGaming

"My Gamertag is OhGoodGaming, and it came about around the time when I first started shooters, I would die SO OFTEN. I would sarcastically yell out "oh good goooood" and it became my Gamertag, eventually I got into Twitch and began streaming, and got incredibly good at games. That's when I thought I should run my same legacy but make it more professional looking hence, OhGoodGaming."

OneUpOrShutUp

"My Gamertag is OneUpOrShutUp. I wanted something that related to retro gaming as it is my true love. I have a huge obsession with the classic Mario Bros games, so it just made sense. I also wanted a name that stood out and had a little sass."

Overtoyou

"Besides being a gamer, I love reading books and interested in XX Century history. Once in my hands appeared the books of genius Roald Dahl about the WWII British Royal Aviation, it contained ten stories about brave pilots and was based on the writer's own experience. Back in the days, I was interested in WWII aviation and this book inspired me so much and became one of my favourite books. The book's name was Over to You. This idiom was used by pilots during radio talks to hand over the initiative in the conversation. Since then, this idiom became my Gamertag."

GAMERTAG BIO

"My story is pretty simple. I'm Australian hence the oz part. I'm an Ozninetieskid in that I was born in the 80s but grew up in the 90s. I love the 16-bit 90s era of gaming. Games like Super Mario World, Sonic the Hedgehog and Zelda a Link to the Past were very influential. I'm also a big fan of 90s music and movies."

Ozninetieskid

"I'm Australian hence the oz part. I'm an Ozninetieskid in that I was born in the 80s but grew up in the 90s."

Super Mario Bros. 3 (NES)

My favourite Mario game of all time, could be my favourite

game full stop. One of the first games I ever played so the nostalgia is strong, but I still play it

to this day and enjoy it just as much. Almost a perfect game in my mind.

The Legend of Zelda: A Link to the Past (SNES)

I love everything about this game. The

music, the art style, the wonderful sense of adventure and exploration, the satisfaction of

solving the puzzles. It is still my favourite Zelda game.

Pokémon Red/Blue (Game Boy)

I still remember getting Pokémon Blue, my first Pokémon

game. It was all-consuming. I would play day and night on the Game Boy and even on TV

using the Super Game Boy. Our school had to ban Game Boys purely because of Pokémon.

While the Pokémon formula was certainly improved on with Gold & Silver, the nostalgia I feel for Gen 1 is too strong.

The Elder Scrolls IV: Oblivion

A truly immersive game. This was my first experience with an

Elder Scrolls game and it is still my favourite of the series. The sheer scale and size of the

open world was breath-taking and experiencing it in first person certainly added to that.

The Witcher 3: Wild Hunt

Stepping away from retro with this one but it needs to be.

on my list. This game was mind-blowing. The graphics were incredible, the story was

gripping, and the world was alive! In my time playing the Witcher 3 I was one hundred

percent invested, to the point where I would lie in bed thinking about the game.

Honourable mentions

Tony Hawk's Pro Skater 3, Grand Theft Auto Vice City, Gran Turismo 2, Super

Mario World, Mario Kart 64.

Twitch: ozninetieskid

Instagram: ozninetieskid

Twitter: OzNinetiesKid

Pago

"It's pretty funny actually, a few years ago I hung out a lot in a big city in Sweden and while there I always drank a juice called Pago. After a while people who didn't know me referred to me as the girl who always drinks Pago. And after that, it became just Pago."

pandasama

"Panda is a family story we love. it's cute, it's noble but it remains a wild animal, decorations in children's rooms and on their clothes. My brother's nickname itself is "Panda Sama," it is logical that I included it in my nickname."

PENT1UMPOOR/ PENTIUMPOOR

"My gamer tag is PENT1UMPOOR (ps4) and PENTIUMPOOR on everything else. I took up the name a while ago because it belonged to an old friend of mine who was a big part of my life growing up. Yeah, she was an online friend, but I talked to her almost daily. Her account ended up getting banned and I lost contact with her. I tried to get in touch with her a while ago but I guess she must have changed her username. I love this name and it brings back a lot of great memories for me. All the time we spent together and how she practically made me who I am now. I miss her dearly and this is my way of remembering her and the time we spent together all those years ago. I guess you could say that, to me, PENTIUMPOOR has a nice ring to it."

PinkCaramel

PinkCaramel, because I love the colour pink and it's a play on my middle name Carmel, as many people point out it sounds like and is spelt like caramel. I've been using it since 2017, I use it on every platform but to name a few, Discord, PSN and Steam.

Pockk_its

"My Gamertag is Pockk_its_ and there's quite a stupid story behind it. I'm a massive Doctor Who fan and have been all my life. My favourite companion is Donna Noble. In her first-ever episode 'The Runaway Bride' she is dressed as a bride when the doctor asks if she has any money. She replies with, "It doesn't have pockets, have you ever seen a bride with pockets, when I went for my fitting at Share's Allison the one thing I forgot to say was, give me pockets!". I absolutely love that line. One of my favourites of all time so I thought it would be some sort of tribute to my favourite doctor and companion."

POLARSTAR

"Hey! I'm POLARSTAR. As a kid, I had a ritual before going to sleep. Every night I would go on the balcony to watch the stars. One day I was thinking I should choose a star, to be mine so I did that...years passed by and I realized that it was the polar star/ north star so the idea to use it as my gamer tag because it's so bright, powerful and...it's mine. I'm also astrophysics passionate so my gamer tag is defining some parts of me."

ProPh3cY^/Froosen

My gamertag witch I use normally everywhere is: ProPh3cY^. It comes from my first online shooter which was Counter-Strike 1.6, I just chose it because of my gaming prophecy, which is... you get shot. I use Froosen now cause it's basically my name and I still get shot?

R3tro.Nerd

"R3tro.Nerd... Just because I'm a collector of old consoles and games."

(Bloodhound, Mirage, Pathfinder from Apex Legends)

(PlayStation 5)

My name is Arina, and I am a game designer. On the Internet, it is better known as rad.vixen. This Gamertag was created from a huge love of video games, as well as because in real life many people call me a Fox, because of my very small stature the abbreviation rad came from my last name. I've loved games since I was a child, and I now make a living from them and creating them.

The Witcher 3: Wild Hunt

I liked this game with its setting and main characters. Herald my love forever.

Half-Life

For me, this game is an incredible classic, over 20 years have passed since its release, and it's still super cool.

The Last of Us

I love the plot of this game, the way people fought through the apocalypse and never stopped believing in their own strength.

Instagram: Rad.vixen

rad.vixen

"I've loved games since I was a child, and I now make a living from them and creating them."

Radar.Shadow

"My gamer tag is Radar.Shadow, I'm in a clan called Radar, before that I used the tag Sharkvictim97, because I was attacked by a shark. I also used to the have the tag SkulkShadow which was from a clan I made, it's a mix between skull and shulk which is short for Shulker, an item in Minecraft."

RafTheWolf7

"My name in Videogames is RafTheWolf7 I picked this name because, Raf is my nickname, the wolf because it is my favourite animal and the 7 because it is my favourite number."

RenagaderTV

My gamer tag is RenagaderTV, I came up with the name as renegade describes someone that rebels, and I forever rebel in games so I added the "er" on the end as to be a Renagader. I changed renEgade to renAgade to make my name more unique. I also added TV in there because I streamed on an Esports TV gaming site.

Retro.avocado.mods

"Retro.avocado.mods. I picked this name because I love retro gaming, avocado and guacamole is my favourite food, and more importantly, it rhymes. People can easily remember it and it is catchy."

RunningEagle

"First of all, I wanted my Gamertag to be strong and empowering, to represent me and women. I started to dig up some empowered historical female facts, but it wasn't enough. I need something that would represent myself more. One woman's story changed everything. Running Eagle, born in Canada in the early 1800s she was a Native American woman. One day she saved her father when he got attacked by an enemy tribe. All the men and her mother didn't approve of her "odd behaviour" playing with boys and dressing like one of them. Her father taught her to hunt and fight. When her parents died, she wanted to go to fight. The leader of her tribe tried to lead her away but failed. She was so successful during the battle that her clan finally honoured her bravery, she was now accepted, and they gave her the name "Running Eagle" She took part in a sacred ceremony reserved for the greatest warriors The first time a woman took part in one of those ceremonies."

SarahBellum93

"Mine's SarahBellum93....a play on my name (Sarah bell) and the cerebellum part of the brain that coordinates motor movements, so it seemed kind of apt."

shaggy1146

"Well, my Gamertag is shaggy1146, the reason for this was I used to have long hair and people thought it was funny comparing me to Shaggy from Scooby-Doo from the movies, I went with it to stop people joking about it, then it became my nickname within my friendship group. I'm called Shaggy more than I'm called by my actual name so when coming to my Gamertag I needed to change it from the random one they give you at first and it was a no brainer to have my nickname. The name Shaggy wasn't available and the suggested one was shaggy1146 so I chose that."

ShesDragonBorn/Chokemedaddy

"My tag for PS4 is ShesDragonBorn. I also play as Chokemedaddy I chose the tag because I thought it would be an excellent troll name plus it's funny to hear the reactions from other gamers mid-game when they realize they're playing with Chokemedaddy."

ShiftyAura

ShiftyAura wasn't initially my Gamertag, it was something ridiculous and randomly generated through my Xbox. I decided to come up with something different, something that best suits me. I stuffer from anxiety so my mood changes with the wind, hence the Shifty part (shift of moods), and an aura is generally associated with moods, hence Aura. Put it together and you get me!

Shooting_Tiger94

"My Gamertag is Shooting_Tiger94 . This is because I had an Xbox account for very long before switching to PlayStation, my Gamertag on the Xbox was "Shooting_Unicorn94," but when I switched from Xbox to PS this username was already taken. I started thinking, I like tigers, my right arm is covered in a realistic lion tattoo. So, every lion needs a strong tiger, because these two animals are two of the strongest in nature. Therefore, I picked the name Shooting_Tiger94 also 94 is my birth year! Shooting was included because I really like shoot 'em up games."

(Apex action)

GAMERTAG BIO

Let me tell you the story of how I was given the name Sir.Prox. "Shadows and Dust" those were the last words of Proximo in the movie Gladiator. Those were the last words of the late great actor Oliver Reed on screen. The old, retired Gladiator, that won his freedom, slave master and head of a gladiator school, that redeemed himself by helping Maximus with his plan of revenge, left such a huge impact on me that I started using the name Proximo everywhere online. A few years later I met my future wife online, she would one day give birth to our two beautiful sons. At first, she only knew me as Proximo or Proxi.

Many years later, I fulfilled a lifelong dream, and we got a dog, seven years old and in desperate need of a new home. The first time I saw him, I knew that he was to carry the name Proximo for the rest of his life. I did not use that name for myself from that day on. Where I went, he went. Proximo was such a charismatic dog that people everywhere wanted to know about him. A good friend started calling him Lord Prox one day. That name caught on and other people started calling and knowing him as Lord Prox. People never asked for my name, which I had no issues with. That was until one day someone started calling me Sir Prox. He just couldn't remember my real name. Admittedly I liked it and other people started calling me Sir Prox as well. From that day on we were known as the duo

Sir.Prox.

"A few years later I met my future wife online, she would one day give birth to our two beautiful sons. At first, she only knew me as Proximo or Proxi."

Lord & Sir Prox. Lord Prox left this life in 2015. I hope he awaits me one day.

Silent Hill

Resident Evil

Mass Effect

Dragon Age

Dead Space

God of War

Bioshock

The Witcher

Assassin's Creed

The Last of Us

Red Dead Redemption

World of Warcraft

Overwatch

Diablo 3

Name: Daniel Ruiz

PSN: Sir_Prox

Instagram: sir.prox

Twitter: Sir_Prox

Sixxinski

"My Gamertag & username for everything is Sixxinski. It came about as I'm a massive Motley Crue fan & I love their bassist Nikki Sixx. I wanted to use the "Sixx" part but that was taken, so I added the "inski" and that's been it for the past eight or so years!"

SlickNick

"SlickNick, I got that nickname when I was about thirteen before my friends started calling me SlickNick my family would call me that because everything that went wrong for me always ended up working in my favour. Whether it be money, sports, games or anything and I would always say "I'm slick with it." The nickname died out a bit, until I got Twitter famous, I did Vine at the time, I had 12.3k followers on Twitter & half million views on my Vine so yeah, that's how I got the name."

SplayBasilisk39

"My Gamertag is SplayBasilisk39 which I've just always liked, no particular reason, unfortunately."

Spontaneouz/ Purple_Weeble

I was an angsty college student, one of my A-Levels was in Art. We were allowed to listen to our Walkman's whilst painting, so I often had Incubus's Make Yourself CD on play. There was a particular song that my angsty-self empathised with - 'Pardon

Me'. Namely the line '..a decade ago I never thought I would be, at 23, on the verge of spontaneous combustion, woe is me.'

Needless to say, this song became my gamertag inspiration. 'Spontaneous combustion' would have been a ball ache to type out whenever I wanted to log in anywhere (this was long before the days of using smartphones to link into the console - this was back in the Nokia 3310 days), therefore I chose the word Spontaneouz. I used Z instead of an S at the end, as Spontaneous was already taken. To be honest, I am glad I made that choice - it looks much better in my opinion.

I have pretty much managed to secure that tag across most platforms, but alas, there have been some (rare) instances where someone has had the same idea as me and taken the Spontaneouz name! So, I have to resort to my backup, Purple_ Weeble.

This name also derives from my college days. The purple element is because I usually had purple dye in my hair. The weeble bit? Well, one day in the common room, my rotund little self nearly fell over a bin. My mates naturally found this hilarious, and because I wobbled a bit as I tried to find my feet, I forever earned the nickname of 'Weeble', because "weebles wobble but they don't fall down." At least I didn't spontaneously combust, I suppose."

Spooky-Roo

"My gamer tag is "Spooky-Roo." At the time of making it, which was probably when I was fifteen, (before that, my brother wouldn't let me make my own profile, so I had to play on his) It was in October I think, so I was in a 'spooky' mood, hence the first part then I used 'roo' as it's the first three letters of my name, so it became Spooky-Roo."

Stephinsitu

"Stephinsitu, Stephanie is my name and I'm an archaeologist. When I excavate, we have paperwork for every layer of soil we bring up. If we happen to find an artifact while excavating one of the questions on our paper is, "Was the artifact found in situ?" If you answer yes, then you found the artifact exactly how it was left hundreds and even thousands of years ago in its original context. It's great when you find an artifact in situ because the soil around it as well as anything else you find near it allows you to interpret what may have happened at the time the artifact was left in its spot. So Stephinsitu means me in my natural environment and the people I know and things I do give context to the person I am."

StoneyBiscuit8

"Here's my Gamertag story: it was 2011 I got my first console the Xbox 360 and I didn't pick a name and I got StoneyBiscuit8 randomly generated; the Gamertag I still have. When I got the Xbox One I transferred the account over, and when I moved to PS4 I also kept is as StoneyBiscuit8."

stuie15

"The PS name is stuie15, and why I picked it was I went a good half a year without a PS3 due to the fat model getting the yellow light of death. By my birthday I had saved up a lot of money to get a new system. However, my old account couldn't be salvaged. So stuie15 was born. It's a combination of a nickname I had and the age I was when I made the account. I wanted to make my name feel very personalised. Even when PS added the option to change the name, I didn't do it, as I felt a part of my life would be gone if I did. It was a new account, started from scratch. New trophies, new friends, new games. It's a part of my life and has always been. I mean in 2021 it'll be my tenth anniversary with that account. I remember because my old console died when I got inFamous 2."

ThatSameer

"My Universal online tag including gaming is, ThatSameer. I picked it around 9 years ago. The username started on Twitter, I wanted something short, snappy and that couldn't be mistaken for anyone else. Imagine someone knows more than one guy called "Sameer" (my name), which Sameer is it? It's ThatSameer. It stuck with me and has been used across every online profile of mine - that way it is universal, and no one can mistake me for anyone else."

The_pink_robin

"The_pink_robin_ Well, I LOVE birds and my favourite bird is a robin, then I just added my favourite colour and so the pink robin was created."

thelastnicko

"I started playing video games a long time ago back in high school. The Pokémon days, Super Mario and Zelda Ocarina of Time were huge at the time. I've been using thelastnicko as my gamer tag for years now. Since my name is Nicolas, I decided to combine that and added: "the last" to make it more of a gamer tag, to me the meaning behind thelastnicko is just a way of saying the last one standing in the game. Sometimes that is not the reality, depending on what I am playing. I have been away from games for a long time but this year I decided to give it a go again. I built a custom setup and am looking forward to this journey again."

Tiny_moth_gaming

"I don't have a cool story to go with mine, I just love moths & think they're cute. Tiny and moth sounded nice together! With my name being Lenon there are no cool nicknames I could have, So I went for Tiny_moth_gaming."

Tokodh

"My Gamertag is Tokodh! I'm a gamer girl from Scotland! I've played all my life growing up with an older brother. Currently, due to funds, my only platform is mobile. Gotta make the best of what you got, right? I have been, and currently, I'm involved with some big and upcoming gaming communities. I got my username from the Game gods!

totallyregularhuman

"So, my Gamertag is totallyregularhuman, I mostly use the short version totallyregular. Why am I called this? Well, until I picked my current Gamertag, I had many different tags like Intel!nside, tlailie "that is my current Instagram name" or even etokroleg which means "this is rabbit" in Russian. Finally, I found out the tag that best describes me. I am not a superstar or an unusual person. I am not a pro player or a good gamer. Just playing as I like, being a totally regular human. Greetings from Russia."

ToxiiicSniperx

"My main Gamertag is ToxiiicSniperx. The reason being is because when I first started playing on Xbox, I played Battlefield Hardline & always picked the sniper class & would get loads of kills. I went into a random Gamertag generator and put in the word 'sniper' and ToxicSniper came up."

TTV_ITZCHARLIE

Hi, my name is Charlie, and this is how I created my Gamertag. I wanted to be a streamer/YouTuber one day, and it took me ages to think of my name. First of all, my YouTube name started as RNLICHARLIE but I didn't get many subscribers, so I changed my name to TTV_ITZCHARLIE on YouTube. My channel grew and now I'm up to the point where I have 235 subscribers and a video that has had 15.5k views. Now I thought of my name by starting my twitch channel and I just put TTV_ITZCHARLIE and that is what I am known as now.

(Taking aim)

(Power up)

"Back when I had just moved out from the house where I grew up, I, of course, realised, as many young people do, that there was no one around anymore to decide what you eat or drink each day. I ended up in a bad habit of eating tons and tons of Twix bars since this was my favourite candy bar at the time. For that reason, I somehow thought I was a fun idea to go by the silly alias "Twixman" online. That stuck for an exceptionally long time, and people even started calling me by that name in real life. With time the internet grew, and more people came up with the same name. As it got increasingly common that this name would already be taken whenever I tried to register myself for a new game or community, I decided to tweak it into something still familiar, but seemingly more unique.

Twixomatic

"I ended up in a bad habit of eating tons and tons of Twix bars since this was my favourite candy bar at the time. For that reason, I somehow thought I was a fun idea to go by the silly alias "Twixman" online."

Castlevania II: Simon's Quest

Although considered one of the most flawed pieces of its entire franchise, this game was my introduction to the Belmont's and their fight against Dracula and will forever hold a very special place in my gamer heart. That cool whipping action, the music, the adventure elements, the general gothic horror atmosphere, and did I mention THE MUSIC? This game set me off on a quest that ended up with adult me buying an unhealthily amount of expensive Castlevania classics.

Super Mario World

I did play all three games that came before this one, despite still not having any video game consoles of my own at the time, but this game set the stage for something new and exciting that would spark my interest in video games in a completely new way. I still find myself humming or whistling the tunes from Super Mario World in the shower, or when I'm out jogging. I also finally ended up buying my own SNES and a copy of this game 25 years later.

The Legend of Zelda: Link's Awakening

Completely ignoring the unforgettable experiences of "A Link to the Past" or "Ocarina of Time", this game probably brought one of the deepest, and most memorable gaming adventures I have ever lived. I was 13 at the time of its release and the Gameboy was the first and still only game console I owned. Having no way of playing the earlier Zelda games, while still eying that third Super Zelda game like a puppy at the dining table, the release of this one meant the world to me. Not only was I actually able to enjoy this adventure, unlike so many other hyped games out there at the time, but it also turned out to be an unbelievably deep and fine-tuned experience, that would suck me in like a portal to another life. I still feel like I experienced this adventure in my childhood. The Switch remake is one of the few collector's releases I have ever spent my dear money on.

Silent Hill 2

Reading a reviewer stating that this game was too scary for him to finish made sure I gave it a try. I hadn't played the first game at the time or even heard about it, but this caught my interest. I don't believe I have ever been so afraid of anything in my whole life as I was of peeking through the apartment doors in those mouldy corridors. We're not even going to talk about Pyramid Head. Strange to think that I kept enjoying returning to this atmosphere so much that I started feeling literal comfort in revisiting the misty horror town. There are few games that I completed as many times as I did this one. And it had multiple endings!

Bioshock

"Would you kindly?" Need I say more? This game, and its sequel, managed to create a world that I still find myself revisiting often, simply for the atmosphere and experience of being there, long after getting over the rollercoaster of a story it first came presented with.

Twitch: DrNostalgo

Instagram: Dr.Nostalgo

UK-Lionheart

"My Gamertag UK-Lionheart. It came from one of my favourite games of all time Final Fantasy 8. My favourite characters final limit, Squalls Lionheart."

Unlimitedretrogaming

The person behind the account is Eric G., 43yo from Ecuador. I started playing since I was very little because my big brother had both Odyssey and Mattel Aquarius systems. Then the Atari 2600 era began, being Plaque Attack my favourite. I received the NES Deluxe Set in 1987 and that's where my video games collecting passion began, keeping most of the games I own as a kid up to this date. In the 16-bit era, I switched to Sega and also played and collected several Genesis titles for many years, including the Sega-CD. I have continued playing and collecting all these years. My favourite genres are adventure, Metroidvanias and shooters. As of the series, my picks are Ninja Gaiden, Castlevania, Zelda, Mega Man, Shinobi, Metroid, Streets of Rage and Gradius.

Wazn

"Wazn - Short form for Wasian. I played competitive Badminton and Table Tennis and received the nickname from that because I'm a white guy. When creating my Xbox gamer tag, Wasian was taken, so I chose Wazn, and it has stuck since."

(Castle of Illusion for the Game Gear)

GAMERTAG BIO

"Okay, so my gamer tag is actually 'whitelion1901'. I choose white lion because of the symbolism of strength and courage; 'a lion never fears the jackal'. It serves as a reminder for me to be strong for others and stay humble. Lions also happen to be my favourite animal and I'm very passionate about conservation issues. The '1901' part is not because I was born in that year, but it is the date that me and my partner got together, and one of my favourite games - Red Dead Redemption 2 - is set around that time.

My full name is Jasmine Newby and my Gamertag is "whitelion1901" (Xbox). My IG name is @whiteliongames and I play games on console and handheld. More notably, PlayStation, Xbox, Nintendo Switch and I also love Arcades! My top five list of games are as follows...

whitelion1901

"The '1901' part is not because I was born in that year, but it is the date that me and my partner got together, and one of my favourite games - Red Dead Redemption 2 - is set around that time."

The Last of Us Part II

The most emotionally impactful game I've played to date. The story really resonated with me personally and I believe everyone should experience it at least once in their lifetime.

The Last of Us

Everything about this game was revolutionary to me when it first released in 2013. The gameplay, soundtrack... it was like nothing I'd ever experienced before, and it immediately had me hooked.

Cyberpunk 2077

Despite its flaws, Night City has my heart. There's nothing more I love then late-night drives through a dystopian, neon-lit metropolis (and hanging out with Judy Alvarez).

Red Dead Redemption II

Can't beat rooting, tooting, cowboy shooting!

The Jak & Daxter trilogy

This trilogy was such a huge part of my childhood and I always find myself going back to it.

Name: Jasmine Newby

Instagram: whiteliongames

xBRASKOx

"My name is Don and I run the gamingwithdaughters IG account. Proud Aussie gamer Dad of three. My Gamertag is Brasko It's also my DJ name, as I would get called it in school, thanks to the awesome Donnie Brasco movie with Al Pacino and Johnny Depp. It was taken on Xbox, so I made it xBRASKOx. I thought it was cool because the first 2 and last 2 letters also spell Xbox which I've been a huge fan of since the beginning."

XxBThoxX

"XxBThoxX. My name is Brandon Thomas, so I took BTho from that and I tried to make it look interesting when I wanted to take the plunge into streaming."

xXg0stXx

"My Gamertag on Xbox is xXg0stXx, I've had it for the past ten years. I was about fifteen when I made it. I don't recall what made me choose this particular pattern of characters for my Gamertag, I just remember coming up with the idea, seeing it on screen and thinking, "That's pretty cool looking!" I've thought about changing it countless times, but I mean I've had it for ten plus years, so I'll just stick with it... for now. Plus, I've never been that great with coming up with cool and creative screen names."

Valravne

My Gamertag is Valravne. I picked this name because I love everything about Nordic folklore and mythology. I also love ravens so much. I saved a baby crow once and taught him many things and let him free after 6 months. His name was Odin. I still miss him so much! After him, I love crows and ravens even more. So I picked the best name for myself. Valravne is a supernatural raven who flies at night, consumes bodies and hearts to gain human knowledge or change his appearance to fool his prays. It is capable of turning into the form of a knight or a half-raven and half-wolf. Valravne was also one of the bosses in Hellblade game. It was great to see it there. They called it the god of illusion. Just like my Gamertag, I love to do tricks to confuse my enemies in games. People call me Val and I feel like it is my second name.

Zenitram Drol

My Gamertag is Zenitram Drol which is Lord Martinez in reverse. Like many, I was into WoW (World of Warcraft) back in the day, and my character was called that, which is just Lord in front of my surname. When I switched to Horde after about a week, I changed it to Zenitram Drol and although I haven't played WoW in almost fifteen years, I have kept using that.

Level 2

Loading...

Printed in Great Britain
by Amazon

58728700R00085